BUILT TO LAST

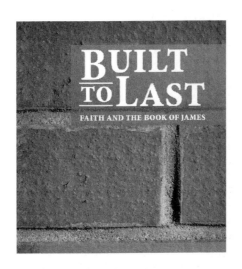

BUILT TO LAST
*Faith and the Book of James*

Greg O. Speck

For video and additional media content please visit
www.gregspeck.com

This book is dedicated to Justin Speck, Julia Speck, Kelley Guske and Garrett Speck. My four children who have taught me what it means to love Jesus Christ and follow Him with a whole heart.

# Table of Contents

# INTRODUCTION

I have always loved the book of James. It is a great book about practical Christian living for today! James is saying to us, now is the time to get up off your big, fat...couch and live for Jesus.

Each day you are going to study one or two verses, so step by step we are going to take a journey through the book of James. I want you to look for what God wants you to start doing, stop doing, and what it means to live for Him.

Use your Bible as you read through this devotional and write some notes in the margins, underline verses and write down what God is saying to you through His Word.

My prayer is that this study will encourage, motivate and help you in your walk with Jesus.

# DAY ONE – JAMES 1:1a

## SOMETHING TO STUDY:

*"James, a servant of God and of the Lord Jesus Christ..."*
James 1:1a

Who is writing the book of James? I hate to start with such a difficult question. How about if I make it multiple choice?

A. Moses
B. David
C. Greg Speck
D. James

If you picked James, then say out loud, "I am the smartest person in the room." Actually, you are probably the only person in the room, but that still makes you the smartest!

So, who is James anyway? He became the head of the church in Jerusalem and was there for Paul's last visit in Acts 21:18. Paul tells us that he was a special messenger in Galatians 1:19, and very influential for the cause of Christ. But it did not start out that way.

James was the brother of Jesus. Jesus was born of Mary conceived by the Holy Spirit and James was born of Mary conceived by Joseph. Imagine being the brother or sister of Jesus. Talk about sibling rivalry! Can't you hear your parents saying stuff like:

"Why can't you keep your room clean like Jesus?"
"Why can't you get good grades like Jesus?"
"Why can't you be perfect like Jesus?"
"Why can't you stand on the water in the bathtub like Jesus?"

This could have been a lot of pressure on Jesus' brothers and sisters. It might have been easier on James if he would have recognized Jesus as the Son of God growing up. Let's face it, you might not mind listening to your older brother as much if you knew he was God. Now, some of your older brothers act like they are God, but trust me they are not. Only Jesus qualifies as being called God in the flesh!

James grew up with Jesus. They ate at the same table, worked in the same carpenter shop and went to the same synagogue. Did James see Jesus as God? I think it is safe to say that there was something different about Jesus, but James did not see Him as the Son of God.

How do I know that? Open your Bible to Mark 3:21 and 31 and read what it says about how his family viewed Jesus. They thought He was mentally disturbed. Perhaps James was teased because of all the crazy things his brother was doing. I can see James trying to help Jesus out during the following incident.

Scene-TURNING WATER INTO WINE

James: "I love weddings don't you Jesus? Everyone is so festive and happy. Hey look, here comes Mom."
*(Enter Mary, the mother of Jesus and James)*
James: "Hey mom. I can't believe they ran out of wine. Someone wasn't thinking ahead. Oh well, I guess…"
*(Jesus approaches water jars)*
James: "Jesus, what are you doing? What are you going to do with these six large jars filled with water? Look, people are starting to stare. We are drawing a crowd."
*(Crowd gathers around Jesus)*
James: "Nothing to be concerned about friends. Jesus is just a little thirsty. Jesus, what are you planning on doing?"
*(Jesus whispers to James)*
James: "YOU'RE GOING TO DO WHAT? I'm sorry, I got a little excited but you can't be serious about turning water into wine. This is crazy and you are going to embarrass this whole family. You are going to embarrass me. Are you listening to me? You don't look like you are listening to me. OK, OK more people are gathering around. Maybe we should go into the kitchen and practice on a glass of water or something. Start small and work up to gallons of water. So how are you going to do this, what is the trick?"
*(Jesus whispers to James)*
James: "What do you mean it's done? Shouldn't you say something magical over the jars?"
*(the master of the banquet enters and tastes the water)*
James: "Ohhhhh, noooooo, they are serving some to the master of the banquet. We will be the laughing stock in all of Cana. I will talk to him and try to distract the crowd. I'll have to stop him

3

from drinking the water, but if I can't then you grab Mom and we can make a run for it."

*(James approaches the master of the banquet)*

James: "Excuse me sir, but my brother has a weird sense of humor and he was playing a joke on you. He was pretending to turn water into...wait don't really drink it because it is only...I beg your pardon?...you say it is delicious?...they saved the best wine for last? But... I mean...you see...I thought...how did He do that?"

James probably spent a lot of time making excuses and apologizing for his brother. To make matters worse, Jesus ended up dying on a cross like a common criminal. Then to top it all off, Jesus was deserted by the twelve men He had poured three years of His life into. This only confirmed to James that his brother was indeed crazy.

Then something happened that rocked James' world. Jesus Christ, his crazy brother, rose from the dead. Read 1 Corinthians 15:7 and you will discover that Jesus appeared to James. What a meeting that must have been! We don't know what was said or what happened during this encounter, but James was radically changed. Jesus went from being his crazy brother to his Lord!

James wrote this book that was named for him and how does he start the book? "James, a righteous Pharisee, you may now lay prostrate before me, the brother of Jesus Christ, who I knew was God from the beginning. I was His favorite brother and He learned a lot from me. I have included the things I have taught Jesus in this book."

No, read again what he said, *"James, a servant of God and of the Lord Jesus Christ."* After growing up with this man, he now acknowledges that Jesus Christ is the Son of God. Hindsight is 20/20, and James now realized that there was something very, very different about his brother Jesus. Although James held a very important role in the church, it was his relationship with God and Jesus (as a servant!) that mattered most to him.

What matters the most to you? Where do you spend your time and what do you think about?

- Money
- Popularity
- Boyfriend

- Acceptance
- Success
- Girlfriend
- Athletics
- Stuff
- Grades
- Music
- Drama
- Looks
- Sex
- (You fill in the blank)

If it's any of these things, you'll never be truly satisfied or happy. While speaking at a school in Florida, I asked a group of girls what they wanted to do with their lives. Their answer . . . we want to make a lot of money. Money is not the answer. You may have tried several of the above options and discovered the same thing. In the end, you are left empty and unsatisfied.

What gives your life direction? What is most important? What gives your life meaning? Just one thing! What is it? The answer is Jesus. There is nothing more important than your relationship with Jesus Christ. When you encounter the living God and He becomes most important to you, then you'll know joy, peace and a purpose that goes way beyond anything the world has to offer.

**God has a purpose, plan and destiny for your life.** Do not live another moment without understanding that truth. He is ready to work in and through your life beyond anything you could ask or imagine.

James discovered that truth and he wants you to make the same discovery. His challenge to us is to live for Jesus—to make Him Lord of your life and follow Him no matter what happens.

## SOMETHING TO THINK ABOUT:

1. Jesus is Lord of all, but is He Lord of your life?

2. Just one thing! What is most important to you?

3. Your yesterdays do not determine your tomorrows. You can be different because the Lord will give you the power to be different. Are you ready to stop playing around and commit your life to Jesus Christ?

## SOMETHING TO PRAY ABOUT:

Start by making sure you have a clear conscience before the Lord. Tell Jesus that you are sorry for any sin in your life. Ask for the Holy Spirit to fill and control you. Now thank Him that you are forgiven and free.

## USE THIS SPACE TO JOURNAL ABOUT WHAT GOD IS SAYING TO YOU:

# DAY TWO – JAMES 1:1b

## SOMETHING TO STUDY:

*"...to the twelve tribes scattered among the nations."*
James 1:1b

To whom is James writing this book? He is addressing Jewish Christians that have been scattered among the nations because of terrible persecution and hardship. What exactly does terrible persecution and hardship look like? Stuff like...

"Do I have to eat another cafeteria meal?"
"Right before prom...a zit!"
"Buford broke up with me."
"Wow, these are bad gas pains."

No way! This was the kind of persecution that most of us will never experience. Those who were committed to Christ were not just killed; they were tortured first and then killed. Nero, a Roman emperor, had Christians covered in pitch, tied to stakes and set on fire to light up his garden parties. Christians were...

- Crucified.
- Fed to wild animals.
- Crushed with huge stones.
- Boiled in oil.
- Fried alive.

Guess what? You didn't have lukewarm Christians back then because it cost you something to follow Jesus Christ. It could cost you your life. Christians did not have the option of sitting on the fence. They were either a follower or they weren't. They were either hot or cold.

James is writing this letter to encourage Christians and to get them involved in service—to tell them that it is worth all the pain and persecution because Jesus Christ is the one true God and their future includes heaven and eternity. He wanted to remind them of both their privileges and responsibilities.

James put his faith into practice and was hated by the Pharisees because of his love for Jesus and his desire to follow Him. They commanded him to deny Jesus and when he refused they took him to the top of the Temple and threw him off. Then they gathered around him and beat him with clubs and stoned him until he was dead.

**My desire is that you would have a deep love and passion for Jesus Christ.** The book of James is a cry against Christians who are hypocrites—against religion that replaces a relationship with Jesus Christ. It is a book that tells you to get up and start living for Jesus! If you study the book of James, you will encounter the one true God and like James you will never be the same again.

## SOMETHING TO THINK ABOUT:

1. Are you living for Jesus or are you sitting on the fence?

2. Are there areas in your commitment to Christ that you are compromising?

3. You are not ready to die for Jesus until you are ready to live for Jesus!

## SOMETHING TO PRAY ABOUT:

Ask God to give you a passion and love for Him and a desire to follow Him no matter what happens.

## USE THIS SPACE TO JOURNAL ABOUT WHAT GOD IS SAYING TO YOU:

# DAY THREE – JAMES 1:2

## SOMETHING TO STUDY:

*"Consider it pure joy, my brothers, whenever you face trials of many kinds,"*
James 1:2

What? This verse makes no sense at all. It would seem to make better sense if the verse said, "Consider it pure joy, my brothers, whenever you get a girlfriend" or "Consider it pure joy, my brothers, whenever everything meets your expectations." But joy and trials just don't seem to go together.

Wait a second, as a Christian I can be joyful because Jesus takes away all of my problems, right? Wrong again. Nowhere in scripture does God ever promise that if you come to Him life will be all rosy, pretty and perfect without any problems. As a matter of fact, He promises just the opposite.

Grab your Bible (I know that you have it, right?) and read John 16:33. What is the promise in that verse? Does it say, "In this world you might have problems, there is a slight chance that something could occasionally go wrong." No, it says, "In this world you WILL have problems." That is a promise we don't like to claim, but it is a promise. If you commit your life to Jesus Christ and follow Him, you will have problems.

I spend half my life in airports flying around the world. There used to be these cult members who would approach people for money. Their promise was that if you committed your life to what they believed you would have no more problems. What a joke! Let's deal with reality. When I would hear that pitch, I'd think, "I've heard that before." Then it hit me. The last time I was in a used car lot someone tried to sell me a car that wouldn't give me any problems. All cars have problems—especially my car! Cars break down and stuff happens. You are going to have problems. The problems that James is talking about are the ones that come out of the blue. They aren't necessarily your fault, but you still have to deal with the consequences.

Imagine borrowing your Dad's brand new BMW to take your friends to Burger King. After a quick bite, you come outside and discover that the driver's side door is caved in…how are you going to react?

Imagine going Christmas shopping for this wonderful person who you have been dating. You know that this is probably the one because it has lasted for five whole weeks. You find the perfect present. It is expensive, but they're worth it because you just love them so much. The day after Christmas they call you, break up and begin to date your best friend…how are you going to react?

Imagine working all year to make the team. Not only do you make the team, but you are also in the starting lineup. Three days before the first game you break your ankle and are out for the season…how are you going to react?

Imagine being in the middle of the biggest test of the year. The person next to you asks how you spell flunking. The teacher sees you say something, accuses you of cheating and flunks you…how are you going to react? Maybe a better question is how should you react? James gives you the answer…REJOICE!

How can you be joyful in the worst of situations? The key is to understand where the joy comes from. The joy does not come from the trial itself. For example, you are playing center field and there is a fly ball coming in your direction. The sun gets in your eyes. The ball passes between your glove and hand, hits you in the nose and breaks it. At this point, you don't say, "Thank you Jesus that my nose is smashed and I am now deformed." No, the joy doesn't come from the trial. The joy comes from within—from your relationship with Jesus Christ and the knowledge that He is in control and I can trust Him completely.

- All joy is found in Jesus Christ.
- If you are a Christian, Jesus dwells within you.
- So the source of all joy is within you.

The joy you experience is not based on circumstances. It is based on your relationship with Jesus Christ. So, you can be joyful no matter what the situation. When you choose to rejoice and be thankful, that's a choice you make, you are saying to God…
- trust you.
- I believe that you can take the worst of circumstances and work them for good.

10

- Please release the Holy Spirit to work in and through me.

If you believe that God is in control and you have trusted Him with your eternity, you can trust Him with today!

You cannot control your circumstances, but you can control how you will respond to those circumstances. Your attitude is crucial. **The trials that you face will either make you better or bitter and it all depends on how you respond to the problem.**

If we treat trials and problems as enemies to be avoided at all costs, we will turn to whatever will help us deal with the pain and disappointment. We turn to things like drinking, drugs, cutting, sex, etc. At best, the relief is only temporary and often instead of helping with the trial it only makes it worse and we end up getting bitter.

When you face trials with joy you'll learn more about yourself, grow closer to Christ and develop as a Christian. You will become better because of the problems.

Do you approach life from the positive or negative? Here is a funny story that I heard years ago and I don't know where it comes from. It isn't true, but it makes a point.

A mother is at her wits end and takes twin boys to a psychiatrist. She tells the doctor that one boy is always a pessimist and the other is always an optimist. No matter what happens one boy complains and the other rejoices. The psychiatrist says that he has an idea and whispers it to the mom. Christmas morning arrives and the two boys are led to a building and each is placed in a different room. The mom and psychiatrist wait twenty minutes and then approach the rooms. They open the first door and there is the pessimist surrounded with the most wonderful toys imaginable. The mom says, "Honey, what did you get for Christmas?" The little boy says, "Nothing good, I hate everything." The psychiatrist scratches his head in amazement and says, "Let's see what has happened to your other child." They open the door and the optimist is standing knee deep in manure with a shovel and he is digging with all his might. Mom asks, "Honey, what did you get for Christmas?" The little boy said, "A horse if I can ever find it!"

**SOMETHING TO THINK ABOUT:**

1. Do you choose to rejoice when trials come your way?

2. Think of the last trial you faced. Did you allow it to make you better or bitter?

3. "God whispers in our pleasure, but shouts in our pain." C.S. Lewis

**SOMETHING TO PRAY ABOUT:**

Thank God for your life and ask Him to teach you through your trials.

**USE THIS SPACE TO JOURNAL ABOUT WHAT GOD IS SAYING TO YOU:**

# DAY FOUR – JAMES 1:3

## SOMETHING TO STUDY:

*"...because you know that the testing of your faith develops perseverance."*
James 1:3

Another word for perseverance could be endurance. This is not a weakness or passive quality. It is not saying, "Oh well, I can't do anything about it so I'll sit here and give up." Rather it is vibrant and dynamic; it is staying power and an attitude that says, "I will not give up." Perseverance says, "I see the trials and I am not going to panic. I will be patient and trust in the Lord with all my heart because He is molding me into His image and that takes time."

A trial tests your faith. How shallow and weak is your faith if you give up every time you are confronted with a problem? A problem will show you just how much you trust in Jesus Christ. It is easy to follow Christ when everything is going great, but what happens to your faith when things start to get hard? What happens when the gushy-gooey feelings leave and you do not sense God's presence? Do you persevere or do you give up and compromise?

It breaks my heart to see the number of teens who tell Jesus they love Him with all their heart while at a camp or conference, but a week later, when they are home, they have compromised and given up on their faith. **Nothing of worth or value is ever easy. We need men and women of courage and endurance.**

It sickens me in sports when a player or team gives up when things get hard. I was watching my son Garrett play football. He is a much better player than I ever was even though I was a star in my own mind. The other team had a wide receiver that was very good; he had size and speed. Throughout the first half, we were playing them even, but in the second half, we started to pull ahead. The receiver was obviously becoming more and more frustrated. Our defense was shutting him down.

Mid-way through the second half the receiver did a double move on our safety and went right by him. He was open and it looked like a sure touchdown. The quarterback tried to get him the ball, but the throw was short and our safety was able to catch up and intercept the ball. The receiver walked off the field, took off his helmet and slammed it to the ground. Then he took off his jersey and shoulder pads, threw them aside and sat down on the bench. He had decided to quit.

Do you want to know what I would have done if I was that coach? I would have walked over to him and said, "Not only can you take the rest of the game off, but you can take the rest of the season off." I would have kicked him off the team. No team wants a quitter playing for them. Some of you may be thinking, "That's right, kick the guy off the team. He deserves it. He had a terrible attitude." But have you treated Jesus this way? Have you quit on Him when things have gotten hard?

## SOMETHING TO THINK ABOUT:

1. What do you do when life gets hard?

2. Problems do not cause attitudes; problems reveal attitudes.

3. Are you willing to persevere for the cause of Christ?

## SOMETHING TO PRAY ABOUT:

Tell the Lord that you desire a strong faith so you can persevere through trials. Ask Him to give you the courage and strength needed to remain faithful.

## USE THIS SPACE TO JOURNAL ABOUT WHAT GOD IS SAYING TO YOU:

# DAY FIVE – JAMES 1:4

## SOMETHING TO STUDY:

*"Perseverance must finish its work so that you may be mature and complete, not lacking anything."*
James 1:4

Do you want to be mature and complete not lacking in anything? Then you need to rejoice in your trials and persevere through them. Do not try to run away from the trial, don't give up and don't give in, but wait on the Lord. As you wait, rejoice, because He is teaching you, maturing you and completing you so that you will not lack anything.

What does the not lacking anything mean? Are we talking about cars, money, dates and stuff? No, we are talking about what is happening inside your life. You will be complete on the inside. You will be someone of character, maturity and integrity with a strong faith that does not give up. You will be ready to face anything that the world, flesh, or enemy throws at you.

Right now, by taking time to study God's word, you are giving up instant gratification for a much greater satisfaction of allowing God to develop you into His image. You are becoming everything Jesus created you to be. One of the by-products of this is how you will feel on the inside. You will be at peace knowing that God has it all under control. You will feel good about yourself because you have learned that real beauty is what you are like on the inside.

Some of us never mature spiritually because we are always running from our problems. These people have no inner peace and they really don't like who they are becoming. If you choose to run from your problems and trials, you will go through something like this...

- You grow bitter, which makes you a very angry person.
- You become disillusioned with life and begin to say, "I don't care anymore."
- You lose touch with God. He becomes unimportant and irrelevant.
- You begin to doubt His existence.
- Finally, you turn your back on Him and walk away.

15

You MUST go through the trials and continue to be obedient to the Lord if you are going to reap all the great things that God has in store for you. Do you know what your future holds? No, but God does and He is preparing you now for what you will experience in the future. You can trust Him because He sees your whole life laid out before Him. He sees your yesterdays and He sees your tomorrows. If you let Him, He will lead you!

Our values will determine how we respond to the trials we face and our response has a lot to do with who we will become. If we value comfort more than character, we will run from trials. If we value the material and physical more than the spiritual, we won't be able to consider it pure joy when trials come. **Outlook determines outcome.** So to end with joy you must begin with joy.

Here is a simple formula to help you deal with the trials that come your way. Just remember to face your trials with "CARE."

- **C**hrist
  Seek Christ first, when a problem comes your way don't make the Lord your last resort; instead make Him your first thought. Take the problem to Jesus Christ in prayer (Matthew 6:33).

- **A**ction
  After you have gone to the Lord in prayer, do what needs to be done. God may tell you to stop doing certain things and start doing other things. You need to learn obedience and then be obedient immediately. We are talking about putting feet to your faith and living for Jesus Christ (1 Corinthians 4:20)!

  For example...

  "I don't understand chemistry."

  Step 1-Ask God to help you and give you understanding when it comes to chemistry. Who knows everything about chemistry? God does—so ask Him to help you!

  Step 2-Turn off the TV and begin to study chemistry. Go to your teacher and ask him or her for help. Get someone to tutor you. All of this is action. Do what God is telling you to do so you can better understand chemistry.

16

"I am not getting along with this person."

Step 1-Pray and ask the Lord to mend the relationship. Ask Him if there are things that you need to do differently. Ask Him if there is stuff you need to apologize for.

Step 2-Hit them with a baseball bat . . . oops, that's not right. Don't do that, but instead, go to them and talk it out.

"I am bored in my relationship with Christ."

Step 1 – Tell Jesus exactly how you are feeling. He knows anyway. Then humble yourself and ask the Holy Spirit to fill and control you after you confess any sins that have come between you and Jesus. Ask Him to renew within you the joy of your salvation. Tell Him that you want to love Him with your whole heart!

Step 2 – A healthy relationship with Jesus doesn't happen magically. It is not inherited, but it needs to be cultivated. This means that you need to develop your relationship with Jesus. Spend time in the Word, worship, obey Him and your parents, etc.

- **R**ely
  Now rest in the arms of Jesus and know that He has it all under control. You do not need to be afraid and you don't need to worry. Just be still and know that He is God. He is in control and if He can take care of the universe He can certainly take care of you (Psalm 46:10).

- **E**ndure
  Be strong and courageous as you endure the trials so that God can make you into someone who is not lacking in anything. As you endure trials, choose to rejoice (Proverbs 3:5-6).

Paul Harvey was a master storyteller and in his book *More of Paul Harvey's The Rest Of The Story,* he told this amazing story.

At West Side Baptist Church in Beatrice, Nebraska, choir practice begins at 7:30pm sharp. Members of the choir are expected to arrive early.

Ladona Vandegrift, a high school sophomore, was having problems with her homework. She had some especially hard problems and would be late for practice. She always came early, but not this evening. She was frustrated, but she would learn to rejoice for those hard problems.

Royena Estes and her sister Sadie would also be late because they couldn't get their car started. They will learn to rejoice when their car doesn't start.

Mrs. Schuster was usually ten minutes early to choir practice, but tonight she was detained by an appointment. It was irritating, but she will learn to rejoice when appointments go long.

Herb Kipf would have been on time, but he had a chore he needed to take care of. However, that is okay because Herb is about to learn to rejoice when chores make you late.

Joyce Black was held up by the unseasonably cold weather. Rejoice when it is cold and it makes you late.

Harvey Ahl was late because his wife was out of town and he had to take care of his two sons. Things didn't go as smoothly as hoped but he will rejoice from now on when his kids slow him down.

Pastor Klempel and his wife were always on time, but his watch broke and he didn't realize it. Rejoice when your watch breaks.

Even Mrs. Paul the choir director found her daughter asleep, which was unusual. She was the pianist. By the time her daughter got up and got ready, they realized that they were going to be late. They had never been late before and this would break their perfect record. Mrs. Paul was upset, but God would teach her to rejoice in her trials.

As a matter of fact, not one member of the choir made it on time. At exactly 7:30pm, on March 1, when choir practice was supposed to begin, the furnace ignited a natural gas leak that blew up the church. The explosion occurred right under the choir loft, the EMPTY loft.

How many times has God stepped in and protected you from some sort of disaster that you weren't even aware of. There are a lot of things that can irritate us during the day. Instead of complaining learn to rejoice in the trials.

## SOMETHING TO THINK ABOUT:

1. All sunshine and no rain make a desert. It is through the hard times that we grow and mature.

2. When it comes to sports you aren't called to just start the game, but to finish it. Anyone can start a relationship with Jesus Christ, but it isn't just about starting. You need to finish well.

3. Are you willing to trust the Lord, wait on Him and rejoice so that He can make you complete on the inside, spiritually mature and not lacking anything?

## SOMETHING TO PRAY ABOUT:

I want you to spend all day thanking the Lord. As you do, I bet you will see a change in your attitude. Be grateful for everything that the Lord has done and is doing for you. God dwells in the praises of His people.

## USE THIS SPACE TO JOURNAL ABOUT WHAT GOD IS SAYING TO YOU:

# DAY SIX – JAMES 1:5

## SOMETHING TO STUDY:

*"If any of you lacks wisdom, he should ask God, who gives generously to all without finding fault, and it will be given to him."*
James 1:5

Here we are in the middle of all these trials and temptations. We are commanded to count it all joy, but that is really hard. So what do you do? Ask God for wisdom! Wisdom is not the same as knowledge. Look at the people around you. They know a lot but still do stupid things. Many young men and women graduate from high school intellectually rich, like you, but morally poor, hopefully not like you.

Your friends have all these street smarts and knowledge, but still say and do stupid things. Here are some true examples of stupid things that people have:

Written to Dear Abby:

- "I'm pregnant but my husband is so unfaithful that I am not even sure this is his child."

Written to the welfare department:

- "I'm glad to report that my husband who is missing is dead."
- "I am very much annoyed to find you have branded my son illiterate. This is a dirty lie as I was married a week before he was born."
- "You have changed my little boy to a girl. Will this make a difference?"
- "In accordance with your instructions, I have given birth to twins in the enclosed envelope."

Written in church bulletins:

- "This afternoon there will be meetings in the North and South ends of the church. Children will be baptized at both ends"
- "This Sunday being Easter Sunday, we will ask Mrs. Taylor to come forward and lay an egg on the alter."

- "On Sunday, a special collection will be taken to defray the expenses of a new carpet. All those wishing to do something on the carpet, please come forward and get a piece of paper."

Written to schools:

- "My son is under the doctor's care and should not take P.E. Please execute him."
- "Tom has been absent because he had two teeth taken out of his face."

Written to insurance companies:

- "Coming home I drove into the wrong house and collided with a tree I don't have."
- "The jerk was all over the road, I had to swerve a number of times before I hit him."
- "The telephone pole was approaching fast; I was attempting to swerve out of its path when it struck my vehicle."
- "The pedestrian had no idea which way to go, so I ran him over."

Most of these people are intelligent with a lot of knowledge, but they sound really stupid. You know those kids who are really smart, but make bad choices. What do they need? What do you need? The answer is wisdom.

What is wisdom? **Wisdom is seeing life from God's perspective.** It is making choices and decisions as God would make them. Why do we need wisdom when we are going through trials? Why didn't he just say we needed strength? Because wisdom will allow us to see trials as opportunities to mature in our faith and to grow up emotionally as Godly men and women.

Where do we get wisdom? It comes from God and all we need to do is ask. We don't have to be good enough or work for it; we just have to receive it from Him. As we draw closer to Jesus Christ, not only will we receive wisdom, but there is also a bonus! He will give us knowledge and understanding. How do I know that? Get your Bible and read Proverbs 2:6.

God will give you wisdom if you ask Him, but He also gives wisdom through making good lifestyle choices. Here are four examples, read these verses in your Bible.

- Proverbs 11:2 – With humility comes wisdom.
- Proverbs 13:10 – Wisdom is found in those who take advice.
- Proverbs 29:15 – Discipline will bring wisdom.
- 2 Timothy 3:15 – Studying the Word of God will make you wise.

Wisdom does not just know what is true and right, but it knows how to apply the truth and live out what is right. Wisdom understands that trials are there for our ultimate good and wisdom gains the victory over those trials. So, asking God for wisdom is the way to conquer the trials in your life. You conquer them by growing through them and learning everything God wants to teach you.

## SOMETHING TO THINK ABOUT:

1. Do you have wisdom?

2. Wisdom is more valuable than silver or gold, Proverbs 3:13-14. Do you agree?   What do you spend more time doing, seeking wisdom or seeking money?

3. Have you ever asked God for wisdom? Do it now!

## SOMETHING TO PRAY ABOUT:

Ask God for wisdom. Tell Him that you desire to begin to see life from His perspective. Ask for His wisdom that will give you victory over your trials.

## USE THIS SPACE TO JOURNAL ABOUT WHAT GOD IS SAYING TO YOU:

# DAY SEVEN – JAMES 1:6

## SOMETHING TO STUDY:

*"But when he asks, he must believe and not doubt, because he who
doubts is like a wave of the sea, blown and tossed by the wind."*
James 1:6

When it comes to asking for wisdom, we have a responsibility.
There's something we need to do if we expect to gain that wisdom. We
must believe and not doubt.

God desires to meet our needs and help us grow through the
trials we are facing. He loves us and cares for us deeply. Does 1 Peter
5:7 say cast all your anxiety on Him because He is God? Or cast all
your anxiety on Him because He is in control? No, it says, *"Cast all
your anxiety on Him because He CARES for you."* God cares for you
and wants the very best for you so you can ask, believe, and not doubt.

**Doubt is a tool of the enemy to get your eyes off of the Lord
and focused on your circumstances, problems, trials, and situations.**
Satan is a liar and the father of lies. He wants you to doubt.

- He wants you to doubt the very existence of God.
- He wants you to doubt whether God even hears your prayers. He
  will say to you that your prayers are just bouncing off the ceiling
  and God doesn't really hear them.
- He wants you to doubt God's presence in your life. He wants you
  to feel alone.
- He wants you to doubt whether God can really help you with the
  trial.

Doubt is attacking the very character of God. You are
questioning His ability to take care of you. You are questioning His
sovereignty and His trustworthiness. That is crazy! He is King of Kings
and Lord of Lords. You don't have to doubt because He is God. You
don't have to doubt because He hung the stars in place. You don't have
to doubt because He is the creator of the universe. You don't have to
doubt because He cares for you.

Read and underline in your Bible Jeremiah 29:11. This verse
says, *"For I know the plans I have for you," declares the Lord, "plans*

*to prosper you and not to harm you, plans to give you hope and a future."* Those are His plans for YOU and no amount of trials will prevent that from happening if you will just hang onto Jesus.

To doubt is to be like a wave on the sea being tossed back and forth. You become a person without direction or purpose. Jesus Christ is your anchor that protects you and keeps you standing strong against all the trials that are sent your way.

## SOMETHING TO THINK ABOUT:

1. How hard is it for you to ask something of the Lord without doubting?

2. Why do you doubt?

3. Be strong and courageous because the Lord, your God, goes before you!

## SOMETHING TO PRAY ABOUT:

Thank God for the plans that He has for you. Tell Him that you want to follow Him and love Him. Talk to Him about any doubts that you are having.

## USE THIS SPACE TO JOURNAL ABOUT WHAT GOD IS SAYING TO YOU:

# DAY EIGHT – JAMES 1:7

## SOMETHING TO STUDY:

*"That man should not think he will receive anything from the Lord"*
James 1:7

When you doubt, you shouldn't expect to receive anything from the Lord. Wow! That sounds kind of harsh. How many of us can ask without any nagging doubts? How many of us can ask without wondering in the back of our minds if God is really going to answer? Not many. I'll be the first to admit that I can have doubts when I come to God and ask Him to work in awesome ways. So, is this a catch 22 where I ask God, but then I have these doubts so I never see Him answering prayer? What am I supposed to do and what are you supposed to do?

Take your Bible and check out Mark 9:17-24. Initial here _____ when you've read the verses. Now focus on 9:22b-24, *"But if you can do anything take pity on us and help us." 'If I can'?" said Jesus. "Everything is possible for him who believes. Immediately the boy's father exclaimed, 'I do believe; help me overcome my unbelief'!"*

The key is being honest with the Lord and saying, "God I do believe that you can take care of me and help me through this trial, please help me to overcome my unbelief." **We are all in process, learning and growing in the Lord.** Part of seeing your faith grow is asking God and then seeing Him work in and through you. The more you see Him work the greater your faith becomes so the more you ask Him and the less you doubt. Pretty soon you are coming to the Lord and asking for amazing miracles and not doubting at all.

Do not allow doubting to keep you from seeking after the Lord and following Him with a whole heart. The closer you draw to Jesus the less you will have to struggle with those doubts. We walk with Him one step at a time. Day by day we learn to trust Him more and more.

Maybe there are certain doubts that you keep struggling with over and over again. I talked with a young man that wrestled with the doubt of whether he was really saved. You may be dealing with doubts that the enemy is using to bring you down. I want you to find someone, an older, Godly man or woman, and talk to them. Allow them to listen to you and speak truth into your life. Jesus promises in John 8:32, *"Then you will know the truth, and the truth will set you free."* God wants to set you free from those doubts that haunt you, those doubts that seem to separate you from God and His love. Don't let that happen. Stay close to Jesus by seeking after Him and allowing others to help and encourage you.

If I can help you at all drop me an e-mail at gregospeck@gmail.com

## SOMETHING TO THINK ABOUT:

1. Are you struggling with any doubts right now?

2. Can you ask of God without ever doubting? Probably not, but can you be honest with Him about your doubts?

3. Are you praying enough?

## SOMETHING TO PRAY ABOUT:

What do you want God to do for you? Ask Him for something great, something that only God could do. Tell Him that you believe and ask Him to help you overcome your unbelief. Remember that as you pray He always hears and He always answers. He doesn't always answer the way we wish He would answer, but He always answers prayer!

## USE THIS SPACE TO JOURNAL ABOUT WHAT GOD IS SAYING TO YOU:

# DAY NINE – JAMES 1:8

## SOMETHING TO STUDY:

> *"...he is a double-minded man, unstable in all he does."*
> James 1:8

On the outside, this doesn't look like a very encouraging verse. Although it is not a verse that you would typically underline or claim, it is an important verse for many reasons. First of all, you notice that the "he" in this verse is someone who doubts and has become double-minded and unstable. It is important to remember that this person is here because of the choices they have made in their life. No one has made them double-minded or unstable. They ended up here because of their own life and the choices they made.

Where have your choices led you? How are you doing spiritually? How are you doing emotionally? Have you taken ownership of your life and your faith? I know that bad things happen to all of us, but you have to stop blaming your past for the struggles you are having today. It is your life and your faith and you have chosen to give that life to Jesus Christ. **So, now it is His life and His faith living through you.** Start making the right choices today!

The man in this verse is also the kind of person who lives a life that is up and down. Do you know anyone like this? They are on a spiritual and emotional roller coaster. Some days they love and follow Jesus and other days they totally ignore Him. They go to a camp or a mission trip and love Jesus with all their heart, but then they come home, start dating, and begin to live a life of sin. This person is unreliable, you can't trust them. You can't trust them to live the way they ought to live or act the way they ought to act. It is like this person has two minds, they aren't sure about life or faith. Sometimes they are hot and sometimes they are cold. Sometimes they say "yes" to Jesus and other times they say "no." They believe and then they don't believe. They are unstable and unreliable in their prayer life and relationship with Jesus Christ.

Is this you? Are you a double-minded person and unstable in what you are doing? If so what do you need to do? Make a good choice now and give Jesus your whole heart.

These last few days have shown you why some of us receive so little from the Lord. Either you aren't asking Him or you ask and doubt. You doubt that He can answer your prayers or help you with the trials. In some cases, you even doubt if He is hearing your prayers.

Each day you are going to be facing trials of different kinds. You must ask God for wisdom and believe that He not only hears you, but that He will also show you the way you ought to go and give you the power to learn from and overcome the trial.

## SOMETHING TO THINK ABOUT:

1. **What you are doing today is what you are becoming tomorrow.** If you know that then what are you becoming?

2. Are you double-minded? What do you need to do if you are?

3. No one you date can or will satisfy your deepest needs like Jesus!

## SOMETHING TO PRAY ABOUT:

Tell Jesus that you no longer want to be that double-minded person. Ask the Holy Spirit to fill and control you completely. Surrender your whole life to Him and give Him your whole heart. Tell Jesus that you love Him and ask Him for the power and strength to make good choices starting NOW!

## USE THIS SPACE TO JOURNAL ABOUT WHAT GOD IS SAYING TO YOU:

# DAY TEN – JAMES 1:9

## SOMETHING TO STUDY:

*"The brother in humble circumstances ought to take pride in his high position."*
James 1:9

We are all at different levels when it comes to things like money, houses, cars, clothes, talents, and abilities. It's easy to find someone who seemingly has it better than you. Maybe you know someone you think is better looking, more talented in band, richer, or more athletic. These comparisons are not what should drive and lead us. Is it wrong to have a lot of money? Is it wrong to be a football star? Is it wrong to be first chair? Absolutely not, however, this is not what is most important. The most important thing is what is happening inside your life. This all has very little to do with your situation or circumstances. What James is saying is, "If you love Jesus and are walking with Him, then you can be excited about the (any) humble circumstances you find yourself in today."

Sadly, we do just the opposite. Instead of being content with who we are and what God is doing in our lives, we become jealous of those we perceive as better than ourselves. We compare ourselves to others, which robs us of joy in life and passion for God. We begin to develop an inferiority complex and feelings of inadequacy. This causes us to either withdraw or compromise.

Instead, you need to rejoice in the humble circumstances you find yourself in right now. How can you do that? Humble circumstances will humble you (OR bring you low) and when that happens you step into a high position.

I want you to grab your trusty Bible and match the following verses with the correct statement:

- 1 Peter 5:5: He will guide you in what is right and teach you His way.
- 1 Peter 5:6: God will give grace to you.
- Psalm 18:27: He will save you!
- Psalm 25:9: In due time, He will lift you up.

In other words, if you are in humble circumstances, you should be seeking after the Lord so that God can continue to work in your life. As this happens, you will find yourself in the very high position of being in the very presence of God.

Be happy in your humble circumstances. God is in control and you can trust Him. He is preparing you for the future and what He wants to do in and through you. God is not caught by surprise. He sees you and understands the frustration of being in humble circumstances, but He also knows what is best for you. Nothing is more important than your relationship with Jesus Christ. **When you are living in His presence, then you are truly in a high position.**

## SOMETHING TO THINK ABOUT:

1. God opposes the proud. Never be in a position of opposition to God.

2. Are you content resting in the arms of Jesus?

3. Think of ten things you can thank God for right now.

## SOMETHING TO PRAY ABOUT:

Are you feeling inferior or inadequate about anything in your life? I want you to thank God for those very things that are bothering you. Tell Him that you want those things to pull you closer to Him and ask Jesus to continue molding you into His image.

## USE THIS SPACE TO JOURNAL ABOUT WHAT GOD IS SAYING TO YOU:

# DAY ELEVEN – JAMES 1:10

## SOMETHING TO STUDY:

*"But the one who is rich should take pride in his low position, because
he will pass away like a wild flower."*
James 1:10

God does not accept a rich person because of what they possess or what they have accomplished. The status of a rich person means nothing to God. It would be like trying to impress a Billionaire with a thousand dollars. To a Billionaire, that is just spare change. The bottom line is that riches do not impress God.

Sometimes we spend our entire life climbing this ladder only to discover that it is leaning against the wrong wall. What we thought was so important turns out to not be important at all. We end up killing ourselves to make money so we can buy things that we don't have time to enjoy and to impress people that we don't really like in the first place.

The rich and the high are no better than the poor and lowly. If you are rich in this world, take pride in your low position because you need Jesus just like the poor. All people, no matter what their status, stand before God in need. As a rich person, recognize your need for Jesus.

Why is it so hard for a rich person to come to faith in Jesus Christ? Check out Matthew 19:23-24. We learn two things:

- It is hard for a rich person to get to heaven
- It would be easier for a camel to go through the eye of a needle than for a rich person to enter heaven.

Why is that true? Is it because God makes it harder for rich people to get into heaven or that He does not want them in heaven? No! This is true because a rich person doesn't see their own needs. The richness of their lifestyle blinds them to what is really important and the needs they have inside their own life.

If you are a star, or extremely talented, or have a lot of money, or are working at a great job, then beware. These may be the very things that are keeping you away from knowing and loving Jesus Christ.

31

Life may seem so wonderful that you say, "I don't need Jesus Christ." The person in the low position sees their need. So be thankful that you are lowly on the inside and acknowledge that fact. Those needs you have on the inside are what draw you to God.

I have met very wealthy people who are aware of their lowly position and are amazing men and women of God. If you are blessed with material wealth, talent, or abilities, be sure to use those riches to glorify Jesus Christ. To whom much is given, much is required. **If God chooses to trust you with riches, use them to make Him look good.**

## SOMETHING TO THINK ABOUT:

1. I once heard that groups of people were interviewed, from all different socioeconomic levels, and it was discovered that lottery winners were the most unhappy. What does that tell you?

2. Are you aware of the needs in your life emotionally and spiritually?

3. What impresses man? What impresses God? What should be most important to you?

## SOMETHING TO PRAY ABOUT:

Ask God to make your heart soft and open to Him. Ask Him to make you aware of the needs in your life. Tell Him that you love Him and want to see Him working in and through your life.

## USE THIS SPACE TO JOURNAL ABOUT WHAT GOD IS SAYING TO YOU:

# DAY TWELVE – JAMES 1:11

## SOMETHING TO STUDY:

*"For the sun rises with scorching heat and withers the plant; its blossom falls and its beauty is destroyed. In the same way, the rich man will fade away even while he goes about his business."*
James 1:11

Just as a flower will be destroyed by the scorching heat so one day the rich person will be gone. That person spends his whole lifetime working for those riches and how does it end? He leaves it all behind because you can't take your wealth with you! All the wealth of the world will not impress God or come with you to heaven.

If you have heard this story, stop me. There was a wealthy man and he was about to die. He prayed to God and asked if he could get all his money changed into gold and bring it with him to heaven. God decided that he could do that if he wanted. So the man had all his wealth converted to gold and put in a huge suitcase. When the man died, he went to heaven with the suitcase. Arriving at the pearly gates Peter asked him, "What is in the suitcase?" With great excitement he opened the suitcase and showed Peter. Peter looked down and said, "You brought pavement with you?"

In heaven the streets will be paved with gold. Your wealth will not impress anyone. Do not be concerned about riches; be concerned about what is going on inside your life. 1 Peter 1:24 says, *"All men are like grass, and all their glory is like the flowers of the field; the grass withers and the flowers fall, but the word of the Lord stands forever."* What makes more sense, to commit yourself to riches or to the Lord?

Money can be lost, talent can be snatched away, looks can fade, and circumstances can change for the worse, but the Lord will remain constant. **Invest your life into something you can't lose . . . your relationship with the Lord Jesus Christ.**

Allow the Word of God to speak to you. Read Psalm 91 for yourself. Here is part of what this chapter says about giving your life to something you won't lose . . .

*"He who dwells in the shelter of the Most High will rest in the shadow of the Almighty. If you make the Most High your dwelling-even the Lord, who is my refuge-then no harm will befall you, no disaster will come near your tent. For He will command his angels concerning you to guard you in all your ways; 'Because He loves me', says the Lord. 'I will rescue him; for he acknowledges my name. He will call upon me, and I will answer him; I will be with him in trouble, I will deliver him and honor him. With long life will I satisfy him and show him my salvation'."*

## SOMETHING TO THINK ABOUT:

1. Is what you are living for worth dying for?

2. "He is no fool that gives up what he cannot keep to gain what he cannot lose." – Jim Elliott

3. Who or what is most important to you?

## SOMETHING TO PRAY ABOUT:

Ask God to give you wisdom to decide what is really important. Ask Him to protect you and lead you. Thank Him that Psalm 91 applies to you!

## USE THIS SPACE TO JOURNAL ABOUT WHAT GOD IS SAYING TO YOU:

# DAY THIRTEEN – JAMES 1:12

## SOMETHING TO STUDY:

*"Blessed is the man who perseveres under trial, because when he has stood the test, he will receive the crown of life that God has promised to those who love him."*
James 1:12

Do you want to receive God's blessing? If you said yes, then you need to persevere under the trials of life. You need to stand firm, refusing to give up and living for Jesus no matter what happens. The blessing you gain is for right now here on earth, it is an inward joy and satisfaction. It is a confidence in God that says, "All is well with my soul because it belongs to God." It is this confidence in God that carries you through the trials and problems you face each day.

Do you give up as an athlete when things get hard? You better not, because one of the attributes of a really good athlete is the fact that they never give up! Do you give up on your homework when things get hard? Oops, OK, bad question. **If you are going to succeed in life and in your relationship with Christ, then don't give up.**

If you persevere, you will receive a blessing now and the crown of life after you die. That crown of life is eternal life and that beats anything this world can offer you today.

Crowns were really big back in Jesus' time. You were honored if you received a crown. If you won a major athletic event, you were given a crown of laurel. Competitors would practice their whole lives and do whatever it took to get that crown of laurel. What happened to the laurel after a few weeks? It dried up and fell apart. They couldn't even keep it. All that work was for something that didn't last. The same thing happens today. We give our lives to things that will not last.

Answer this quick quiz. You must do this from memory.

- Who won the World Series four years ago?
- Who won the Superbowl five years ago?
- Who won the Stanley Cup three years ago? (This award was given to the winning hockey team. Perhaps years from now, as

you read this book, there will no longer be hockey. It was a game played on ice where the object was to hurt your opponent.)
- Who was basketball's most valuable player three years ago?
- Who won the mile in the last Olympics?
- Who won Miss America last year?
- Who won Miss Universe two years ago?
- Who was your school Homecoming queen five years ago?
- Who won Miss Prune Pit, who won Name That Rash, who won Karate Dominoes?

In most cases, we don't remember and further more we don't care. It's no big deal to us, but it was huge for deal for them. What happens if a guy walks onto your campus and says, "Eight years ago I was the quarterback for your team!"? Do you really care? Are you overly impressed? I don't think so. We work so hard for stuff that doesn't last. God says that if you will persevere then He will bless you now and give you a crown of Life that will never fade, rot, or decay. It will last forever!

Starting now, I want you to do what is right. Even if everyone in your group does what is wrong you do what is right. Even though they make fun of you, do what is right. Even though they laugh at you, even though they put you down, even if they reject you, do what is right. Be more concerned with the approval of God rather than man. Be more interested in God's opinion of you rather than man's. In the end, who will decide whether you go to heaven or hell? Will it be your little group of friends or will it be the King of Kings? Commit yourself to following Christ and persevering.

What do sheep do really well? They follow the crowd.

- One sheep walks out into the pasture and they all go out into the pasture.
- One sheep comes in for a drink and they all come in for a drink.
- One sheep walks off a cliff and they all walk off a cliff...AHHHHHHH!

Sheep don't really think for themselves. They just say, "OK, here we go over the cliff. Hey, everybody else is doing it. Hope this feels good."

That describes some of us. People say to us…drink that, smoke that, steal that, sleep with that and we say, "OK, everybody else is doing it. Hope this feels good." We become like those sheep that mindlessly follow the crowd and end up over the cliff and messed up.

What will sustain us through the trials and problems? What will give us the courage to stand strong against peer pressure? The promised blessings are nice, but that isn't what motivates us. The promise of eternal life is awesome, but sometimes that seems so far away. It must be our love relationship with Jesus Christ. Knowing that He loves us and choosing to love Him back.

How do you love Jesus? Do you tell Him? That is really nice, but talk is cheap. Have you ever had a boy or girlfriend that told you they loved you but didn't act like it? What speaks louder, their words or their actions? Your actions speak louder and if your actions do not back up your words than your words become worthless.

Get your Bible and read this verse and then underline it. This is Jesus speaking to YOU! What is John 14:15 saying to you? If you are going to love Jesus, then you need to show Him, and you show Him by being obedient; start doing what He wants you to do and stop doing what He doesn't want you to do. Does it sound simple? The concept is simple, but the application is hard because it means changing your lifestyle to live in such a way that you honor the Lord.

If I said to you, "Let's be best friends; you will be my SPECIAL friend." I go out with you and say, "I like you." Then I slap you in the face. A little later I say, "You are my favorite friend." Then I kick you as hard as I can. I say, "I like you a lot." Then I head butt you. Pretty soon you would think, "I don't think he likes me at all." Sometimes we treat Jesus this way, we tell Him we love Him but then we treat Him very badly. What speaks the loudest to Him? If you love Jesus then live for Jesus!

## SOMETHING TO THINK ABOUT:

1. Do you stand against peer pressure or do you allow others to lead you into sin?

2. Are you sure that one day you will receive the crown of life? If you are not sure, e-mail me at gregospeck@gmail.com and I would like to

tell you how you can be sure, without a doubt, that you will go to heaven.

3. Do you love Jesus Christ? Can He tell by watching you?

## SOMETHING TO PRAY ABOUT:

Ask God for the strength to stand against peer pressure. Ask Him to give you favor in the eyes of students at your school so that you can lead them toward the      Lord. Tell Jesus that you love Him.

## USE THIS SPACE TO JOURNAL ABOUT WHAT GOD IS SAYING TO YOU:

# DAY FOURTEEN – JAMES 1:13

## SOMETHING TO STUDY:

*"When tempted, no one should say, 'God is tempting me.' For God cannot be tempted by evil, nor does he tempt anyone."*
James 1:13

What is temptation? It is a desire and longing to do what is wrong, to do something that God has told us not to do, or to do something that is going to hurt us or someone else, emotionally, spiritually, or physically.

Sometimes those temptations, those cravings, seem unbearable. We say to ourselves, "This is what I want and I want it now and I don't care what the consequences are going to be for me in the long run." We see something that we want, we know it is wrong, but the desire is so strong that we can hardly stand it. What do you crave that God forbids?

- Pornography
- Cutting
- Getting drunk
- Drugs
- Being Prideful
- Pre-marital sex
- Overeating
- Hating
- Lying
- Cheating
- Gossiping
- Stealing
- Chasing furry little chipmunks (maybe that is only a temptation for me)

You could add a lot to this list. Temptation is an individual thing and what tempts you may not tempt your friends. But all our temptations share these three things in common; they disobey God, they look really good and they hurt us.

The things we are tempted to do feel good either physically or emotionally. If they didn't feel good, then we wouldn't do them. For example, not many of us would be tempted to do this: Walk into the kitchen and grab the butcher knife. Move to the cutting board and place your hand, fingers extended, on the board. Now cut off your fingers. Not many of us would be tempted to do this because we would say, "That doesn't feel good!" But not everything that feels good is good for us. Some of the things that feel the very best to us right now can be causing us tremendous problems and pain.

Remember, just because the world says something is OK doesn't mean it is OK. God defines sin, not the world, and no amount of approval from the world makes sin anything but sin.

When we are tempted, we want to play the blame game. "It's not my fault that I did this bad thing. Everybody else is to blame, but not me." Today, no one wants to take responsibility for their actions. It is easier to blame the past, family, friends, or your circumstances rather than saying, "It is my fault and I choose to do it." If I blame others, then I don't have to feel guilty. This blame game comes naturally to us and can be traced back to the garden.

God makes this wonderful, amazing place called Eden and says to the man, "All this is for you. Go where you want to go and do what you want to do. Eat from whatever you see, but just do this one thing. Do not eat from the tree of the knowledge of good and evil."

To make a long story short, Adam and Eve look at the tree and it looks pretty good to them. They are tempted to eat of the tree, they give in to the temptation, and they eat from the one tree God asked them not to eat from. What were they thinking for crying out loud?

God confronts Adam and asks him, "Did you eat from the tree that I commanded you not to eat from?" To which Adam immediately takes responsibility for his actions, NOT, looks God right in the eyes, and says, "The woman YOU put here with me--she gave me some fruit from the tree and I ate it." Adam is blaming God. If you hadn't given me the woman, then she wouldn't have given me the fruit, and I wouldn't have eaten it.

God turns to the woman and says, "What is this you have done?" She answers, "The serpent deceived me and I ate." Eve blames the serpent for her bad choice.

Both Adam and Eve are trying to pass the buck for their sin. But whose fault is it that these two committed this sin? It's their fault. When you sin whose fault is it? It's your fault!

I am tempted to think Adam, you idiot, why did you do something so stupid. You were living in paradise and you threw it all away to eat from this one tree? That makes no sense! But then God reminds me that I do the same thing. He gives me life abundant, pours out His blessings, longs to hang out with me, answers my prayers, and promises me a crown of life, but I give in to temptation. I see something and I know that I shouldn't do it and I do it anyway! Whose fault is it when I give into temptation? Is it your fault when Greg Speck does something stupid? NO, it is my fault!

God will never tempt you to do evil. He loves you, cares for you, and desires what is very best for you. I would never tempt any of my children to do anything that is evil and wrong. I know that there are sick parents today that do lead their children into evil, but a parent that truly loved their child would never do such a thing. If I, who make bad choices and give into temptation want what is best for my children then how much more will a holy and perfect God want what is best for us? You can trust God with your life and be confident that He will never lead you into evil.

Plus, God can't be tempted to do evil. It is beyond Satan's ability or power to tempt God. So because He is not tempted by evil, we can come to Him and know that He is our rock, anchor, and stronghold in times of temptation. In Him we will find no evil or temptation. **Jesus will keep you from sin or sin will keep you from Jesus.**

The truth is that you are not out of control. You do not need to give into temptation. Satan would lie to you and tell you the temptations are too strong and no one could possibly stand against them. But that is a lie. You can make good choices now and you can withstand temptation as you trust God completely and surrender your life to the control of the Holy Spirit.

## SOMETHING TO THINK ABOUT:

1. What are your greatest temptations?

2. What are you doing about those temptations?

3. Spending time with Jesus and sharing your struggles with others are two of the best things you can do to combat temptation.

## SOMETHING TO PRAY ABOUT:

Talk to God about the temptations that you are struggling with and ask Him for the strength and power to not give into them. Ask Him to lead you away from the temptations.

## USE THIS SPACE TO JOURNAL ABOUT WHAT GOD IS SAYING TO YOU:

# DAY FIFTEEN – JAMES 1:14

## SOMETHING TO STUDY:

*"but each one is tempted when, by his own evil desire, he is dragged away and enticed."*
James 1:14

Where do those temptations that slam us so hard come from?

- The World

Every time we watch TV we see commercials that try to tempt us with wonderful things like…

- A combination weed wacker/fruit juicer
- The tummy sizer, thigh buster, butt slicer exercise machine
- The "You can be a millionaire overnight" success seminar for only $999.99

But they also tempt us with terrible things. The world has discovered that sex sells so commercials use sex to sell everything. Watching TV today fills our minds with all kinds of images that lead us toward temptation.

- Satan

Just by observing us he can see the areas that we are weak in and he is always looking for opportunities to lead us away from God. His desire is to pervert and destroy all that God has created.

Do not be ignorant of the fact that you have an enemy who wants to bring you down through temptations. Get that trusty Bible and read 1 Peter 5:8-9 and see what it says about your enemy the devil.

- Wake up and realize what is happening. You must be self-controlled and alert. Be alert to the temptations that the enemy will send your way and be self-controlled to stand against the attack.
- The devil is a roaring lion and he would like to devour you. That seems kind of scary but the reality is, *"Greater is Jesus Christ that is in you than the enemy that is in the world."* The

devil will try to intimidate you, but he can't touch you as long as you stay in the center of God's will for your life.

- Instead of being scared you need to resist him and stand firm in your faith. The victory is already yours, but you need to claim it.

Your own evil desires are the source of a lot of your temptations. It is time that you understand and own up to that fact. Sometimes your biggest enemy is yourself. You are tempted when you are drawn away from God by your own evil desires. Where do these evil desires come from that are pulling you away from God? They dwell inside of you. How did they get inside of you? You let them in through your eyes, ears, and mind.

What you take into your life either strengthens you against temptation or makes your more susceptible to temptations. If you fill your mind with sexual and sensual images, then you will struggle with lust of the flesh. If you listen to music that is hostile and negative, then you will struggle with anger. Lust begets lust, anger begets anger, and sin begets sin. What you put into your life is exactly what comes out of your life for good or for bad.

You look or think about something that is forbidden or harmful and you begin to lust. You start to focus on what you should not look at and think about what is forbidden by God. You desire to go after these things and this is the beginning stage of temptation.

Is being tempted a sin? No, we are all tempted to seek after things that we shouldn't go after. How do I know that being tempted is not a sin? Check out the example of Jesus by getting your Bible and reading Hebrews 4:15. This verse tells us that Jesus was tempted in every way just like we are and yet He did not sin. Temptation is not a sin; the sin comes when we give into those temptations and evil desires.

Men, you are sitting in a coffee house when a VERY good looking woman walks in. You can't help seeing her and that isn't the problem. What is the problem? The second look, which is accompanied by lusting as you check out her body and allow your imagination to run wild. Remember that Matthew 5:28 says, *"But I tell you that anyone who looks at a woman lustfully has already committed adultery with her in his heart."* Here is a wise old saying, "You can't stop a bird from flying over your head, but you can stop it from making a nest in

44

your hair." You can't help the fact that you are going to see things that will tempt you, but you can decide not to dwell on them.

There is a battle that is going on inside of you between your old nature and your new nature. Your old nature wants to give in to the temptation while your new nature desires to please God.

Charles Spurgeon said, "There is a battle inside my life between my old nature and my new nature and it's like two big dogs that are constantly fighting." Someone asked him, "Which dog wins?" His answer was powerful, "Whichever dog I feed the most." If you feed your old nature then your old nature will win, but if you feed your new nature then your new nature will win. Which nature are you feeding?

Check out Galatians 5:16-17, which says, *"So I say, live by the Spirit, and you will not gratify the desires of the sinful nature. For the sinful nature desires what is contrary to the Spirit, and the Spirit what is contrary to the sinful nature. They are in conflict with each other, so you do not do what you want."* These are choices that you have to make. Will you gratify your sinful nature or will you live by the Spirit? This is not rocket science. You become your own worst enemy when you make bad choices to look at, listen to, and think about stuff that is gratifying your sinful nature.

D.L. Moody was asked, "Who has given you the most problems in your lifetime?" He responded, "The person that has given me the most problems is D.L. Moody."

We are all under attack from the world and the devil, but perhaps your worst enemy has been yourself. Start doing something about that right now. **The choices that you are making now are creating a future for you.** Is it a good future or are you headed in the wrong direction? It's not too late, so live to please Jesus Christ.

## SOMETHING TO THINK ABOUT:

1. What are you taking into your life? Is it helping or hurting you in your war against temptation.

2. Who is to blame for all the bad decisions that you have made?

3. It is time for you to grow up and take responsibility for your faith and commitment to Jesus Christ. This can't be the faith of your Mother or Father or Youth Pastor. This must be your faith.

## SOMETHING TO PRAY ABOUT:

Ask God to open your eyes to the evil desires inside of your life. Ask Him to make you sensitive to the things that you are watching, reading, listening to, and doing. Ask Him if there are things that you need to stop doing so that you can experience more victory in your life.

## USE THIS SPACE TO JOURNAL ABOUT WHAT GOD IS SAYING TO YOU:

# DAY SIXTEEN – JAMES 1:15

## SOMETHING TO STUDY:

*"Then, after desire has conceived, it gives birth to sin; and sin, when it is full-grown, gives birth to death."*
James 1:15

It all starts with a thought, "I know it isn't right, but this is what I want." Next, it moves to an action. After a while, those actions lead to a lifestyle of sin, which eventually leads to death--spiritual, emotional, and sometimes physical death.

The enemy never gives you a blueprint or complete picture when it comes to sin. You see someone very attractive and you want to be with that person. You want to be intimate with him or her emotionally, spiritually, intellectually, and sexually. You begin to think about the possibility of sleeping with this person.

When you actually start to entertain the possibility of doing something wrong, then sin is being conceived in your mind. You begin to play the fantasy over and over again in your mind. At this point, you have given birth to sin. How do I know that? Check out Matthew 5:28, what does that say to you?

But it all sounds very romantic and exciting to you. You ignore God's still small voice that is whispering truth to you and instead you listen to the enemy. You listen to the enemy who is screaming though the raging hormones and garbage that you have been exposed to and he reminds you that . . . "a lot of teens are having sex and if you use protection you will be fine. Nobody will know and besides, you know that you will be spending the rest of your life with them because they are the one". So after thinking about having sex and giving birth to sin, you put feet to your sin and decide you will sleep with this person. It all sounds wonderful up to this point, the perfect fairytale come true. You have played with the sin and allowed it to mature, becoming full-grown. It now gives birth to death, much to Satan's delight, and reality paints an ugly picture for you. Imagine the following happening...

- You are having this funky itching and burning so you go to the doctor and discover you have a sexually transmitted disease.

47

- You keep having sex, but it isn't as romantic as the first time. As a matter of fact, you begin to feel used and it all starts feeling very wrong.
- A couple of months after becoming sexually active, you discover you are going to be a parent even though you used protection.
- Now your other half decides to end the relationship even though they swore to you that they would always love you.
- Someone talks to someone who talks to someone else and pretty soon everyone knows what happened.
- Your parents are shocked because they thought you could be trusted, your Youth Pastor has to remove you from leadership in the youth group, and your close Christian friends seem to be looking down on you.
- Pretty soon you have these feelings of depression, regret, anger, self-hate, guilt, loneliness, and fear. All you thought you would ever feel is love. Your relationship with God is non-existent.

Did the enemy know something like this would happen? Yes, because he has seen it happen thousands of times in the past. He offers you something that looks good on the outside knowing that eventually it will lead to death.

Stay away from sin. *"For the wages of sin is death, but the gift of God is eternal life in Christ Jesus our Lord,"* Romans 6:23. **Sin will kill you, but God desires to give you life now and life eternal.**

God has given you natural desires about what you see, hear, feel, smell, and taste. The enemy seeks to pervert what God has created so you allow your own evil desires, assisted by the devil, to lead you away from what the Lord desires. You are aware of something that is forbidden and instead of fleeing from it you begin to move toward it. In your mind, you picture the pleasure and conceive desire. You begin to lust after those desires and sin is born. Now your heart is set to think or do what is forbidden by the Lord. The sin grows and gives birth to death. You may never actually carry out what you are fantasizing about, but you probably would if you had the opportunity.

Starting now, you need to put 1 Thessalonians 4:4-5 into practice, *"That each of you should learn to control his own body in a way that is holy and honorable, not in passionate lust like the heathen who do not know God."*

48

This is all about you and the direction that you are heading in your life. Decide that you will not settle for anything less than God's very best for your life. The truth is that you are not some animal that is out of control. You can choose to do what is right and what will honor God. Those who live in passionate lust end up miserable, lost, and on death's doorstep.

Instead, you must learn to control your body in a way that is holy and honorable. That is a life that pleases God and a life that will lead you to joy, peace, and fulfillment. Remember that you don't have to make bad choices. You can choose to walk away from sin. No one can make you do something that is wrong. God will give you the strength, power, and wisdom to make the right decisions. Read Philippians 4:13, *"I can do everything through him who gives me strength,"* and underline it in your Bible. That is a promise for you to claim. When temptation raises its ugly head, you claim that promise and know that you can walk away without giving into the desire and sin that lead to death.

I believe in the power of God working in and through the lives of teenagers. No one loves Jesus like a teen loves Jesus and no one follows the Lord like a teen follows the Lord. I have a conviction that you are the generation that God is raising up to fulfill the Great Commission and bring Jesus Christ to every tribe and nation. So learn now to walk away from evil desires so He can prepare you to be a hero of the faith.

## SOMETHING TO THINK ABOUT:

1. Who do you listen to--the world, Satan, your desires, or God?

2. Have you listened to your desires and done what is wrong? How did it end up? Are you learning from your mistakes?

3. God wants what is very best for you so why wouldn't you follow Him?

## SOMETHING TO PRAY ABOUT:

Tell God that you desire to honor Him today. Tell Him you want to live in a way that brings a smile to His face. Ask Him to reveal any sin in your life and then tell Him you are sorry and that you will turn away from anything that dishonors Him.

**USE THIS SPACE TO JOURNAL ABOUT WHAT GOD IS SAYING TO YOU:**

# DAY SEVENTEEN – JAMES 1:16

## SOMETHING TO STUDY:

> *"Don't be deceived, my dear brothers."*
> James 1:16

To be deceived means that you are listening to lies or allowing others to lead you astray. What are some of the ways that you are being deceived?

You are deceived if you think that other people are responsible for the bad choices you are making. It is so much easier to blame others for a messed up life than to take responsibility for your own life. That way you don't have to feel guilty about the choices you are making because it isn't your fault.

"It's my parent's fault because they are so strict. If they would have allowed me to do more stuff then I wouldn't have rebelled and made all these bad choices."

"It's my teacher's fault. If he wasn't so boring, I wouldn't have acted rudely and gotten in trouble."

"It's my coach's fault. She never lets me play so I am not going to listen to her. She doesn't know what she is doing so I talk when she is talking and I get in trouble. That wouldn't happen if I had a good coach."

"It's my girl/boyfriend's fault. If she/he hadn't pressure me, I would have never had sex."

"It's my parent's fault. If they weren't so lenient, I wouldn't have gotten involved in all that sin."

"It's Satan's, the world's, my brother's, my sister's, my cousin's, my great grandmother's, the dog's, my hamster's, Ronald McDonald's fault. But it isn't my fault."

We want to blame anybody and everybody except ourselves. When we do that, we are being deceived. Whose fault is it when you mess up? It is your fault! **You must take responsibility for your own life and the choices that you make.**

You are deceived if you think that God is playing cosmic games with you and putting you into situations where you are being tempted. God is your best friend and your biggest advocate. He desires what is best for you and He wants to see you succeed spiritually.

The enemy would want you to believe that God doesn't really care, that He is playing games with you, moving you toward sin, and not there when you need Him the most. Those are all lies and you are being deceived.

Stop listening to the lies and decide to follow Jesus Christ. He will give you the wisdom to avoid deception and the strength to do what is right. No one loves you like Jesus loves you so it only makes sense to commit your life to Him!

## SOMETHING TO THINK ABOUT:

1. What does it mean for you to own your life?

2. In what areas are you being deceived?

3. Follow God and live life to the fullest.

## SOMETHING TO PRAY ABOUT:

Ask God to give you the strength to admit that you have messed up and ask Him to give you the power to begin to make good choices. Tell Him that you will be obedient to whatever He asks you to do today.

## USE THIS SPACE TO JOURNAL ABOUT WHAT GOD IS SAYING TO YOU:

# DAY EIGHTEEN – JAMES 1:17

## SOMETHING TO STUDY:

*"Every good and perfect gift is from above, coming down from the
Father of the heavenly lights, who does not change like shifting
shadows."*
James 1:17

I want us to check out three major points in this verse. There
are some great things for us to talk and think about.

- Every good and perfect gift comes from above!

God is good and perfect so He is the source of all good and
perfect gifts. He desires to give those gifts to you. What are the two
characteristics that you notice about the gifts that He is going to give to
you?

- They are good. They are good for you and will help you to
  grow and mature so that you become everything God has
  created you to be. God's good and perfect gifts will not lead
  you into temptation or evil.

- They are perfect for you. That means they are exactly what you
  need at just the right moment. He knows you better than you
  know yourself so He can give what is perfect for you. Have
  you ever picked out the perfect gift for someone and been so
  excited to give it to them? That is how God feels. He has
  picked out the prefect gifts for you. They are exactly what you
  need and they will be good for you. Now keep in mind that the
  gift may not be what you want, but it is what you need.

Who knows better what a two year old needs, the Mother or the
two year old? If the two year old had his way, he would only want to
eat ice cream and chocolate. Mom knows what is best for the child, so
the child ends up eating vegetables because that is what he needs even
though it isn't what he wants.

Who knows best what you need, God or you? God knows what
is best and gives you what you need even though it might not be what
you want. **Remember that God is always more interested in your**

**character than He is your comfort.** So what He gives you isn't always easy or fun, but it is good and perfect for you.

God wants to give you a joy that circumstances and situations can't take away. His good gifts will give us confidence in Him and assurance that all is under His control. We find security, love, and peace in the good and perfect gifts that He gives us. A friend can give us a purse or a football, but only God gives us a love that never fails. There are some awesome gifts waiting for you.

Get your Bible and read these verses: Psalm 18:30, Psalm 34:8, and Nahum 1:7. The Lord is good! You can trust Him to want what is very best for you. When is the last time you prayed for something you needed, but didn't necessarily want? In some cases…never! I am not talking about outward stuff like cars and popularity, but rather inward qualities. Have you ever prayed for your character, faith, integrity, patience, kindness, etc.? Those are things you really need.

- He is the Father of the heavenly lights

Temptation is the path to sin that leads you into darkness. Some of you are in darkness right now being surrounded by feelings of self-hate, depression, guilt, shame, disgust and I am sure that you can add more feelings to this list. Darkness is a secret place where you sin and you don't think anyone sees you. Darkness is a mind surrendered to the enemy. Darkness is emotions out of control. Darkness is acts of evil.

*"But the way of the wicked is like deep darkness; they do not know what makes them stumble,"* Proverbs 4:19.

*"Woe to those who call evil good and good evil, who put darkness for light and light for darkness, who put bitter for sweet and sweet for bitter,"* Isaiah 5:20.

*"This is the verdict: Light has come into the world, but men loved darkness instead of light because their deeds were evil. Everyone who does evil hates the light, and will not come into the light for fear that his deeds will be exposed. But whoever lives by the truth comes into the light, so that it may be seen plainly that what he has done has been done through God,"* John 3:19-21.

The light that has come into the world is Jesus Christ. Too many teens love sin more than they love Jesus so they stay in the dark. They choose to do evil and end up hating Jesus Christ. Don't you see that at school? There are students who hate the name of Jesus and you wonder why? It is because they are living in darkness. However, if you love the Lord then you move toward the light and allow others to see how God is working through you.

God is the creator of the sun, moon, and stars. God is light and in Him there is no darkness. He shines brightly and the darkness cannot stand against Him. We are a choice away from being free from our own personal darkness.

*"You, O Lord, keep my lamp burning; my God turns my darkness into light,"* Psalm 18:28.

*"Even in darkness light dawns for the upright, for the gracious and compassionate and righteous man,"* Psalm 112:4

*"For you were once darkness, but now you are light in the Lord. Live as children of light (for the fruit of the light consists in all goodness, righteousness and truth) and find out what pleases the Lord. Have nothing to do with the fruitless deeds of darkness, rather expose them,"* Ephesians 5:8-11.

Ask God and He will move you from darkness into His wonderful light. He will set you free from the chains of sin and set your feet upon His solid rock. If you are living in the light, what will be coming out of your life? Goodness, righteousness, and truth are the fruits that you should be experiencing in the way you live your life and relate to other people. That kind of life pleases the Lord!

- God does not change.

Have you ever had a friend that was very moody? They change from hour to hour. One minute they are happy and the next they are upset about something. It is confusing and uncomfortable to be with them because you never know how they are going to respond and act. With God, you don't have to worry about Him acting one way today and then totally different tomorrow. He is the same yesterday, today, and tomorrow. There is a lot of security in trusting your life to a God who is solid and consistent.

## SOMETHING TO THINK ABOUT:

1. What do you need, not necessarily want, in your life?

2. Are goodness, righteousness, and truth coming out of your life?

3. You can depend on God no matter what happens.

## SOMETHING TO PRAY ABOUT:

Thank God that He never changes and that you can depend on Him. Ask Him to give you something that you really need. Pray that He would produce goodness, truth, and righteousness in your life.

## USE THIS SPACE TO JOURNAL ABOUT WHAT GOD IS SAYING TO YOU:

# DAY NINETEEN – JAMES 1:18

## SOMETHING TO STUDY:

*"He chose to give us birth through the word of truth, that we might be
a kind of first fruits of all he created."*
James 1:18

The birth that James is talking about occurred when you asked
Jesus Christ to become savior and lord of your life. The word of truth is
God's word, the Bible. The great news is that God chose to save us; He
didn't have to and no one made Him. Why did He do it? He wanted to
see us move from darkness into light. There is nothing we have done to
earn, deserve, or be worthy of His love. That alone should cause us to
worship Him!

Since He gave birth to us, we are now His children and once
you are a child you can't all of a sudden not be a child. That parent-
child relationship can never be changed. A birth cannot be undone. You
will always be your Mom and Dad's child just like you will always be
God's child if you have received Him into your life.

The first-fruits of a harvest were offered to God in thanks for
how He had provided for their needs. Plus, they were saying, "All the
harvest belongs to you God and we understand that without you we
would have nothing. So receive this offering that acknowledges that
everything belongs to you."

So we, too, belong to God and we offer ourselves as a sacrifice
to Him. We say to Him, "Everything that we have and all that we are is
because of what you have done in our lives. I offer myself to you!"

Read Romans 12:1, *"Therefore, I urge you, brothers, in view of
God's mercy, to offer your bodies as living sacrifices, holy and
pleasing to God-this is your spiritual act of worship."* God has blessed
us, provided for us, loved us, forgiven us, saved us, and adopted us as
His sons and daughters. What else would we do but offer ourselves to
Him as living sacrifices?

**I confess that without Jesus Christ I would be nothing.** My
righteousness would be like filthy rags, my mind depraved, my actions
self-promoting and my eternity lost. I owe Him everything--my life, my

service, my love, and my future. All the gifts that I possess, all the talents that I use, and my very breath come from Him. I have nothing to boast about except…

*"But, let him who boasts boast in the Lord. For it is not the one who commends himself who is approved, but the one whom the Lord commends,"* 2 Corinthians 10:17-18.

*"May I never boast except in the cross of our Lord Jesus Christ, through which the world has been crucified to me, and I to the world,"* Galatians 6:14.

How about joining me in offering your life to Christ completely?

## SOMETHING TO THINK ABOUT:

1. God chose you to be His child! How does that make you feel?

2. Has there been a time in your life when you invited Christ into your life?

3. Have you offered your life to God as a living sacrifice?

## SOMETHING TO PRAY ABOUT:

Praise and worship Him, tell Him that you will be a sacrifice for Him to use any way He wants. Acknowledge that without Him you would be nothing.

## USE THIS SPACE TO JOURNAL ABOUT WHAT GOD IS SAYING TO YOU:

# DAY TWENTY – JAMES 1:19

## SOMETHING TO STUDY:

*"My dear friends, take note of this: Everyone should be quick to listen, slow to speak and slow to become angry,"*
James 1:19

Take note of this, pay attention, what I am going to say next is important. That is what God is saying through James. Everyone is to do these three things.

Everyone should be quick to listen.

This is directed toward you because you are someone and this is for everyone. If you are going to grow in your relationship with God and fulfill His plan for your life, then you must listen to the Word of God. If we are going to understand the people around us, then we must learn to listen. How can you really know someone unless you know their heart, and how can you know their heart unless you spend time with them and listen? Some of you reading this right now talk too much. Is that you?

Listening is key to all relationships, but it doesn't come natural to a lot of people. Most people would rather talk than listen and most would like to talk about themselves. Listening is important to God and it should be important to you. Get your Bible and read Luke 10:38-42. You read about a conflict between two sisters, Mary and Martha. Martha is running around trying to get things ready for Jesus and His disciples. Mary comes and sits at the feet of Jesus. What does Jesus say to Martha at the end of the story? *"Mary has chosen what is better."* What did she choose? She chose to sit at the feet of Jesus and listen to Him. It is hard to hear the voice of God if you don't take the time to listen. When is the last time you waited for the Lord to speak to you in silence? Try it sometime, it is really hard. You need to practice so that your mind does not wander like crazy, but it opens the door for the creator of the universe to speak to you.

Slow to speak.

Are you slow to speak or are you the first one that runs off at the mouth? Do you try to become the center of attention by being funny or appearing really smart? Are you mister know-it-all or the expert on every subject? By the way, people that think they know it all really bother those of us who really do know everything!

Here is a good phrase to live by: **make sure that brain is turned on before putting mouth into gear**. Proverbs 10:19 says it like this, *"When words are many, sin is not absent, but he who holds his tongue is wise."*

Like riding a bike or throwing a ball is something that you learn, so is listening. If you are a listener, then you will be highly valued and sought after by others that are looking for someone to care. Plus, you avoid saying really, really stupid things. Allow me to share some examples:

- "Venezuela! Great, that's the Italian city with the guys in the boats, right?" Murad Muhammad boxer
- "A zebra cannot change its spots." Al Gore
- "Nobody in football should be called a genius. A genius is a guy like Norman Einstein." Joe Theismann commentator and former quarterback for the Washington Redskins
- "Smoking kills. If you're killed, you've lost a very important part of your life." Brooke Shields
- "Left hand, right hand, it doesn't matter. I'm amphibious." Charles Shackleford-played basketball for North Carolina State.
- "I would not live forever, because we should not live forever, because if we were supposed to live forever, then we would live forever, but we cannot live forever, which is why I would not live forever." Miss Alabama 1994 in the Miss USA contest answering the question, "If you could live forever, would you and why?"

Slow to become angry.

One of the problems with angry people is that they have stopped listening. They are so busy trying to get their own way that they no longer are sensitive or even care about others. You become like a bull in a china shop. You lash out doing a lot of damage with your tongue. You speak and act without thinking and end up doing things that you later regret.

When you are angry you are no longer hearing God's voice. You are missing out on golden opportunities to learn and grow. When you are angry and have stopped listening for God's voice you become like a blind man swinging a sharp sword. You are just lashing out and hurting people around you and sometimes you are clueless to the impact that you are having.

Is God telling you to never be angry? No, there are times for anger and it can motivate you to positive action. But there is a rule for your anger that you find in Ephesians 4:26-27, *"In your anger do not sin. Do not let the sun go down while you are still angry, and do not give the devil a foothold."* You can be angry just don't sin. How do you do that? Check the object of your anger and your motivation. Is the object of your anger something sinful and wrong or are you mad at someone because you don't like something they said or did? Is your motivation for the anger to right the wrong and bring healing to a situation or is it revenge and winning an argument?

Why do we get angry? Let me give you four reasons for anger.

- It's not fair, you feel that you have been ripped off. I once flew into Atlanta to change planes to get home to Chicago. The plane arrived late into Atlanta, but my plane to Chicago was still at the gate. When I arrived, I learned that they gave my seat away because I was late getting to the gate. I told them I was late because of their plane and they didn't care. I got angry!
- Your expectations have not been met. You expect a person to act a certain way and when they don't you become disappointed and frustrated which can soon lead to anger.
- You have been hurt. Hit your thumb with a hammer and it HURTS. Do you say, "Thank you Jesus for this wonderful experience?" No, usually you get angry. That is also true when you are hurt emotionally. Someone dumps you and that can lead to anger.
- Sin in your life. You feel guilty and bad but instead of dealing with the sin you lash out at others.

If I am going to be sensitive and understand others, if I am going to be able to hear God's voice, then I must be quick to listen, slow to speak, and slow to become angry.

## SOMETHING TO THINK ABOUT:

1. Do you talk too much?

2. Do you have an anger problem? What have you done to get some help?

3. Slow to speak, slow to become angry and quick to listen. Which one do you need to work on the most?

## SOMETHING TO PRAY ABOUT:

Ask God to make you a listener today. Ask Him to bring some individual into your life that is hurting so that you can care.

## USE THIS SPACE TO JOURNAL ABOUT WHAT GOD IS SAYING TO YOU:

# DAY TWENTY-ONE – JAMES 1:20

## SOMETHING TO STUDY:

*"for man's anger does not bring about the righteous life that God desires."*
James 1:20

Anger is not a characteristic that is highly valued by God. Did Jesus ever get angry? Yes, read John 2:12-16 about when He cleared the moneychangers out of the temple. However, there are big differences between Jesus' anger and ours. Let me point out just one area. Read John 2:15 and tell me what Jesus does right before He drives out all the moneychangers. Now think about why this is significant.

Jesus walks into His Father's house and finds men who have turned the temple of worship into a circus. If He was like me, He would have exploded immediately and ended up sinning. Instead, Jesus sits down and makes a whip. How long does it take to make a whip? It takes a significant amount of time. He has to find the materials and then He has to make it. During that time, Jesus is able to calm down emotionally and think the whole thing through. When Jesus walked back into the temple to clear it, He was under control emotionally and He had a plan.

A big difference between righteous anger and anger that leads to sin is whether your emotions or intellect is in control at the time. If your emotions are in control, then you are heading for sin and that kind of anger does not bring about the righteous life that God desires for you. Now, I am not suggesting that if you are angry with a friend that the first thing you should do is make a whip. What I am saying is that you need to calm down and think the whole thing through.

**God wants you to live and experience a righteous life and an angry person does not please the Lord.** Listen to what God has to say to you in Proverbs about being angry.

14:17 *"A quick-tempered man does foolish things, and a crafty man is hated."*

21:19 *"Better to live in a desert than with a quarrelsome and ill-tempered wife."*

63

22:24-25 *"Do not make friends with a hot-tempered man, do not associate with one easily angered or you may learn his ways and get yourself ensnared."*

29:11 *"A fool gives full vent to his anger, but a wise man keeps himself under control."*

29:22 *"An angry man stirs up dissension, and a hot-tempered one commits many sins."*

A righteous life is one that honors the Lord and sets a good example. Anger does not fit into that lifestyle. When you are angry, you end up committing many sins. You push people away from Jesus rather than draw them closer. You do not make Jesus look good.

## SOMETHING TO THINK ABOUT:

1. What makes you angry?

2. Does your anger lead to a righteous life?

3. What do you need to do so you don't get so angry?

## SOMETHING TO PRAY ABOUT:

Ask God to remove from you an angry heart. Ask Him to speak to you if you begin to become angry. Tell Him that you want to live a righteous life that pleases Him.

## USE THIS SPACE TO JOURNAL ABOUT WHAT GOD IS SAYING TO YOU:

# DAY TWENTY-TWO – JAMES 1:21

## SOMETHING TO STUDY:

*"Therefore, get rid of all moral filth and the evil that is so prevalent and humbly accept the word planted in you, which can save you."*
James 1:21

In this verse, the whole idea is to take something off and get rid of it. You are out playing mud football and now you are going to take a shower. The first thing you do is take off all of the muddy clothes. In the same way, get rid of the last little bit of moral filth. Whatever is making your soul and spirit dirty needs to be thrown away.

Notice that the evil is prevalent. What does that mean? It is all around you and very easy to find on any given day. If drugs are prevalent at your school, then it is easy for you to buy drugs. If parties are prevalent at your school, then it is easy to find a party to go to on the weekend. Sin and evil are prevalent and very easy to find. You must get rid of the evil and filth if you are going to be able to hear God's voice and know what He wants you to do.

**Sin makes you deaf to the voice of God.** Students always want to know what God wants them to do for their future. The problem is that they are involved in all kinds of filth and evil so they are deaf to what the Lord would like to say to them.

Instead of the evil, humbly accept the Word of God that is already planted in you if you're a Christian. You are not to be demanding. Don't tell God what to do and don't brag or boast about what you can do for God. Instead, sit at His feet and humbly receive whatever He wants to tell you. When you humbly accept the Word, it means you are willing to act upon it and do what God is asking you to do. It also means that you are willing to stop doing what God is asking you to stop doing.

The Word planted in you is going to save you now and for all eternity. It will save you now from the filth and evil that is everywhere and it will save you in the future so that you will live in heaven with God forever!

How do you get rid of the filth and evil? Take these steps right now.

- Read 1 John 1:9. Confess your sins and God will forgive you and cleanse you. He is the one that makes you clean and gives you a brand new beginning. You can never go so far that the Lord can't reach you. All you need to do is reach out to Him and you will discover that He is reaching back to you.
- Ask God if there are things that you need to get rid of and then listen. I am not preaching book burning, but if He is asking you to throw away some stuff like music, pictures, magazines, DVDs, posters, clothes, and other stuff then just do it! Get rid of anything that dishonors the Lord.
- Ask the Holy Spirit to fill and control you. Surrender every area to Him. Tell Him to take control of your mind, body, tongue and emotions and He will do it.

## SOMETHING TO THINK ABOUT:

1. It is easy to sin, but hard to live for Jesus.

2. Is there any filth or evil that you need to get rid of right now?

3. You won't hear the voice of God if you aren't listening.

## SOMETHING TO PRAY ABOUT:

Ask the Lord to reveal any filth or evil that you need to get rid of right now. Tell Jesus that you want to hear His voice and if He will speak you will listen and be obedient.

## USE THIS SPACE TO JOURNAL ABOUT WHAT GOD IS SAYING TO YOU:

# DAY TWENTY-THREE – JAMES 1:22

## SOMETHING TO STUDY ABOUT:

*"Do not merely listen to the word, and so deceive yourselves. Do what*
*it says."*
James 1:22

It is good to go to church and listen to the Word being preached.
That is wonderful and I encourage you to continue. But if you think
that listening to the Word and knowing what is says is all that is
required of you then you are WRONG. I know teens that can quote
scripture and explain deep truths of the faith to me, yet they are living
in sin. **Today you mark your Bible, but does your Bible mark you?**
Are you being changed by the Word of God? For that to happen, you
need to do what the Word is telling you to do.

To think that you are doing fine by just going to youth group
and listening to your Youth Pastor is to be deceived. You must be
living for Jesus Christ on a daily basis. When you read the Bible or
listen to a sermon, you will hear commands--things that God is asking
you to do. What do you need to do when you read or hear the command?
You need to be obedient.

Christianity is about action, stepping out in faith and living
what you believe. Your friends need to see that Christianity is practical
and that it works. They are attracted to Jesus Christ and Christianity by
seeing the reality of Him in your life.

Today we have students that listen to the Word every week and
then go out and live life the way they want to live it. They live just the
opposite of what they profess to believe. What do we call these people?
They are called hypocrites. We all hate hypocrites, but we have all been
hypocrites at some point in our lives. Stop living a lie. If you believe in
Jesus, then live for Jesus.

Satan seeks to deceive you. He wants you to believe that it is
just fine to live the way you want to live as long as you go to church
once a week. He is happy to have you involved in leadership at your
youth group--talking from the front, playing in the worship band, even
praying. It is OK with him if you read the Bible as long as you don't
apply it to your life. He will seek to develop pride in your life. He will

whisper in your ear, "You are doing just fine. Everyone parties and messes around. Look at all the good you are doing at church. One day, when you get older, then you can really commit yourself to God."

You listen, believe, become deceived, and your walk with Jesus is pathetic. You are apathetic about the things of God. You are a spiritually obese Christian. You feed upon the Word but you never exercise your faith. You do not apply or live out what you are hearing and reading.

It is not good enough to just hear the Word of God but you must apply it and live it out in your life.

## SOMETHING TO THINK ABOUT:

1. A hypocrite is someone who believes one way and acts another. Are you a hypocrite?

2. What has the enemy been whispering in your ear?

3. Commands are in the Bible for you to obey!

## SOMETHING TO PRAY ABOUT:

Ask God to point out commands in scripture and tell Him that you will be obedient. Ask Him to point out any deception in your life.

## USE THIS SPACE TO JOURNAL ABOUT WHAT GOD IS SAYING TO YOU:

# DAY TWENTY-FOUR – JAMES 1:23-24

## SOMETHING TO STUDY:

*"Anyone who listens to the word but does not do what it says is like a man who looks at his face in a mirror and, after looking at himself, goes away and immediately forgets what he looks like."*
James 1:23-24

Imagine that you are out on a date with the person of your dreams. You go to a very romantic restaurant, kind of like Burger King with candlelight, and you are having a wonderful time. Right after dinner you excuse yourself to go to the bathroom. After taking care of business, you step to the sink to wash your hands. As you wash your hands, you glance in the mirror and notice that you have big greasy mark across your face. Do you say to yourself, "Oh no...I can't believe it...it is beginning to smear...oh well, I'll take care of it tomorrow." Even if I don't know you, I would go out on a limb and guess that would not be your reaction. Instead, you would glance in the mirror and say, "AHHHHHHHHHHH!" You would grab the soap, paper towel, hand cream, moisturizer, and nail clippers, anything that might get that mark off your face. You aren't going back into the restaurant with that mark. If you couldn't get it off, you would send a note to the person saying, "Sorry, caught the plague and had to go home."

But don't we do that with God's Word? We read something and God touches our heart. We see something we need to change, do differently, or get rid of all together. We close our Bible, walk away, and forget what we just read. We are like the man who looked at his face in the mirror and forgot what he looked like.

Do you remember what I said earlier? Life is a process and we are making the changes and corrections that we need to make day by day. God is seeking to mold us into His image. That will never happen if you keep forgetting what you are reading in His word. You must be applying the truths of scripture on a daily basis.

Plus, if you do not practice what you learn, you forget what you learn. The things you read will quickly fade from memory. You don't put it into practice later on because you have forgotten what you are supposed to do. **Apply the Word immediately and it will make an impression that you will not quickly forget.**

69

How stupid would it be to look at your face in the mirror, notice that your hair is moving in directions that you thought were impossible, and not do anything about it? It is just as dumb to look into the Word of God and hear the Lord speaking to you but decide that you are not going to do anything about it—to just walk away and forget it. Similar to a mirror, the Word of God shows us what we really look like on the inside.

## SOMETHING TO THINK ABOUT:

1. When you look in the mirror and see things that need to be taken care of, like a big white-headed zit, do you take care of it immediately? What about things that God points out in your life that need taken care of? Do you do it immediately?

2. God is preparing you for your future. Are you learning?

3. Read the Word and apply it and you will grow in your relationship with Him.

## SOMETHING TO PRAY ABOUT:

Ask Him to help you to see yourself clearly like a man looking in the mirror. Ask Him to bring to the surface all the areas that He wants to work on. Tell Him that you want to apply His Word to your life.

## USE THIS SPACE TO JOURNAL ABOUT WHAT GOD IS SAYING TO YOU:

# DAY TWENTY-FIVE – JAMES 1:25

## SOMETHING TO STUDY:

*"But the man who looks intently into the perfect law that gives freedom, and continues to do this, not forgetting what he has heard, but doing it – he will be blessed in what he does."*
James 1:25

Take note of these six things . . .

- You need to look intently into the Word of God. That means study, dig into, and look deeply at what God is saying to you. When you were little, it was fine to read a verse and say a quick prayer, but as you mature you should be spending more time in the Word and digging deeper. I suggest that you read less but go deeper. For you to study three verses and to really know what those verses mean is better than reading a whole chapter and not getting much out of it.

- The Law is perfect and you can trust it. You can trust it to be true and you can trust it to be looking out for what is best for you. The Law comes from a perfect God that deeply loves you. The Law does not exist to hurt or abuse you. Just the opposite, the Law directs you to avoid those things that would hurt and bind you. God's plan from the beginning was to give you paradise. He has already begun to work on your final dwelling place, in heaven, with Him. It will be more wonderful, beautiful, and exciting than anything you could ever imagine. I have seen the birth of my four children and it was WONDERFUL . . . but heaven will be more wonderful. I have stood in Switzerland, among the Alps, and it was BEAUTIFUL . . . but heaven will be more beautiful. I watched my San Francisco 49ers win Super bowls and it was EXCITING . . . but heaven will be more exciting. What are some wonderful things that have happened to you, beautiful sights you have seen and exciting moments in your life? Heaven will be a billion times better! If you have trusted your eternity to God, then you can trust Him today to look after you and direct you through His perfect Law.

- This perfect Law that you are studying gives you freedom. It is freedom from the bondage of sin and death. The world would like to put you in a box and control you, but God wants you free to live life to the full. Your soul and spirit longs to be free from the chains of sin. Remember when you made those commitments at camp, a youth conference, or mission trip? It felt so good to be free of the sin and you were so happy. Your soul and spirit were singing for joy and you sensed that deep down inside. But then you went back home and back to what your body craved and soon you forgot about that commitment. The result of going back to the sin was to experience a life of misery with occasional highs. **If you study the Word of God on your own, then you can experience the freedom that you truly long for deep down inside.** You don't need an emotional experience or a spiritual high. All you need is the living God working in your life.

- Do not forget the lessons that the Lord is trying to teach you. Initially, He will try to teach you through the perfect Law and let you know what you should and shouldn't do. If that doesn't work, then He will allow life to teach you and that can be much harder because it involves some bad choices, stupid mistakes, and emotional pain. If you don't learn what He is trying to teach you, then He will continue to put you in situations that will bring to the surface the things you need to learn. Do you want to learn the hard way or the easy way? It is up to you, but I would suggest the easy way. Remember what God is saying to you though His Word and apply it to your life. Do what He wants you to do and stop doing what He doesn't want you to do. You can read something in the Bible, believe it, tell others about it, write a paper about it, but until you have applied it to your life, you haven't learned the lesson.

- So do what the Law is telling you to do and you will reap a harvest of righteousness. You will feel great about yourself, your conscience will be clear, and you will have a good reputation in the eyes of others. Worry and anxiety will no longer rule your life and you'll have a peace that passes all understanding.

- Do you want to be blessed in what you do? Well, here is a promise that you can claim. Study the Word of God, don't forget what it says, but apply it to your life and you will be blessed in what you do. God will open the ministry doors, give you favor, and bless your socks off. What is sweeter than the blessing of God? Nothing beats having the Creator of the universe approving of you and laying His hand of blessing on your life.

Here is some of what you will experience . . .

- Freedom to discover your destiny and become all God has created you to be. Freedom to refuse to settle for anything less than God's very best.

- Having purpose in your life right now and the hope of heaven in your future. Knowing that with Jesus the best is always yet to come.

- You will have a confidence and security of knowing that you are in the center of God's will and you are experiencing His protection. There is no place safer than the arms of Jesus Christ.

- A deep down joy that is not dependent on circumstances. During the day you will find yourself smiling for no good reason except that you are receiving God's blessing.

You could add so much more to this list but that alone is enough to make me long for God's blessing in my life. What does the world give that compares to what God gives? Nothing! But still Satan whispers lies and has us believe that stuff or people will be better than the blessings God would give us. How stupid is that?

Romans 2:13 says, *"For it is not those who hear the law who are righteous in God's sight, but it is those who obey the law who will be declared righteous."*

1 John 2:17 says, *"The world and its desires pass away, but the man who does the will of God lives forever."*

The Word of God is so great and wonderful. It is the very words of God Almighty speaking to us personally. Don't miss out on the blessings of God by ignoring His Word. The Word of God will change your life!

## SOMETHING TO THINK ABOUT:

1. Do you study the Word of God?

2. Are you learning the lessons that God is trying to teach you?

3. Have you experienced the living God pouring out His blessings on your life?

## SOMETHING TO PRAY ABOUT:

Ask God to give you a love for His Word, the perfect Law. Tell Him that you will be obedient to what you study and ask Him to speak to you.

## USE THIS SPACE TO JOURNAL ABOUT WHAT GOD IS SAYING TO YOU:

# DAY TWENTY-SIX – JAMES 1:26

## SOMETHING TO STUDY:

*"If anyone considers himself religious and yet does not keep a tight rein on his tongue, he deceives himself and his religion is worthless."*
James 1:26

Wow, just shoot me through the heart. Here is an area that God is speaking to me about right now. My tongue can be my downfall. I think that I have the gift of sarcasm, but my wife has made it clear that sarcasm is not a gift of the Spirit. When I get mad, I say things that I later regret. Do you ever struggle in this area? Here are some areas that we might fall short in when it comes to the tongue. See if you fit into any of these categories.

- Talking too much and dominating a conversation. Everyone else has to listen to you, but you aren't listening to anyone else. Do you interrupt other people when they are speaking so that you can tell a story?

- Being an angry person and attacking others verbally. You become cruel, rude and insulting. You don't care if what you say hurts someone else and in some cases you hope it does hurt.

- Are you a gossip? Now that hurts, doesn't it? So many teens struggle with gossip. Gossip is making someone look bad in someone else's eyes. I have heard some individuals say that gossip must be lies. No, gossip can be truth or lies, but you are making someone look bad by what is coming out of your mouth.

- Profanity, swearing, blasphemy, and crude jokes. Swearing is so crude and shows a lack of creativity on your part. People say to me that they are only words and are not that big of a deal. True, they are only words, but what we associate with those words is a big deal and it can become very offensive. The worst form of swearing is blasphemy and that is taking the Lord's name in vain. This means that you are using the King of King's and Lord of Lord's name as a filler or profanity. Do you know what they used to do with people that blasphemed in the Old Testament? They would kill them! Never say, "Oh my God" or "Jesus Christ, I couldn't believe what they did." Even if you don't believe in God, have more respect than to use God's name in vain. Please read Matthew 12:34-37 and then watch what is coming out of your mouth and especially how you use God's name.

- Being a negative and critical person. For you the cup is always half empty and you always find something to complain about. People will get tired of you real fast. Most people I know do not like hanging out with someone who is negative, whiney, and complaining. We as Christians have a lot to be thankful for and rejoice in so lets stop being so negative.

Proverbs talks about the tongue a lot. Here are a few samples . . .

*"Put away perversity from your mouth; keep corrupt talk far from your lips."* 4:24

*"The wise in heart accept commands, but a chattering fool comes to ruin."* 10:8

*"When words are many, sin is not absent, but he who holds his tongue is wise."* 10:19

*"A gossip betrays a confidence but a trustworthy man keeps a secret."* 11:13

*"Reckless words pierce like a sword, but the tongue of the wise brings healing."* 12:18

*"The Lord detests lying lips, but he delights in men who are truthful."* 12:22

*"He who guards his lips guards his life, but he who speaks rashly will come to ruin."* 13:3

*"The tongue that brings healing is a tree of life, but a deceitful tongue crushes the spirit."* 15:4

*"A man of perverse heart does not prosper; he whose tongue is deceitful falls into trouble."* 17:20

*"A gossip betrays a confidence; so avoid a man who talks too much."* 20:19

*"He who guards his mouth and his tongue keeps himself from calamity."* 21:23

Did God speak to you at all through Proverbs? I know He did to me. We both need to work on our tongues. If we don't do this, then we deceive ourselves and make our religion worthless. Is that important? Yes, it is very important. **We deceive ourselves by thinking that God doesn't really care about what comes out of our mouths.** The enemy would like to tell you that it doesn't matter and it is nobody's business what kinds of words you use.

As we have seen, God cares a lot about what is coming out of our mouths. The sad fact is that we make our relationship with Christ look worthless if we aren't keeping a tight rein on our tongues. We actually end up driving people away from Jesus Christ.

Do what I do and ask the Lord to put a guard on your lips. Read and underline Psalm 141:3, *"Set a guard over my mouth, O Lord; keep watch over the door of my lips."*

Ask God to convict you if you're about to say something that He doesn't want you to say. If you are serious about this and will be obedient, then the Lord will do that for you.

I have asked the Lord to do that for me. There have been times when I have prepared to say something either from the front or to someone personally and the Lord has said to me, "Don't say that!" If I am obedient, then He will continue to speak to me. However, if I ignore Him and say it anyway, then I have found that He will wait until I am ready to be obedient before He tells me to not say something again.

We both need to work on our tongues. If we claim to be Christians and do not ask God to control our tongues, then we deceive ourselves and we make Jesus Christ look worthless in the eyes of others. It is a great privilege to be a Christian, but it is also an awesome responsibility. By our words we make God look very good or by our words we make God look very bad. Our words can validate our relationship with Jesus Christ or it can cause people to think that what we believe is worthless. Words are important!

## SOMETHING TO THINK ABOUT:

1. Is your mouth getting you in trouble?

2. Do you think that your words usually draw people closer to Jesus or drive them        farther away from Him?

3. If bad things are coming out of your mouth, then what does that say about what is going on in your heart?

## SOMETHING TO PRAY ABOUT:

Ask God to convict you of anything that is coming out of your mouth that does not please Him. Ask Him to put a guard on your lips and tell Him that you will be obedient and keep your mouth shut as He reminds you.

## USE THIS SPACE TO JOURNAL ABOUT WHAT GOD IS SAYING TO YOU:

# DAY TWENTY-SEVEN – JAMES 1:27

## SOMETHING TO STUDY:

*"Religion that God our Father accepts as pure and faultless is this: to look after orphans and widows in their distress and to keep oneself from being polluted by the world."*
James 1:27

This study is all about living for Jesus and putting feet to your faith. We all ought to have a desire to serve the Lord in any way we can. So what can you do that would be pure and faultless? God has some suggestions for you.

Look after orphans, those who have no parents because of death or some other circumstance. Abortion is the road to death and adoption is the road to life. The United States used to have a lot of orphanages, but now we find most are overseas. If you have never visited an overseas orphanage, I highly recommend you take that step. There are several mission organizations that target orphanages. Will it break your heart? Yes, but you will be loving the way God has called you to love. It will be a sacrifice that the Lord will accept as pure and faultless.

Take care of widows in their distress. How long do we think widows suffer? Most churches would say about two weeks because that is how long we bring hot dishes and look in on them. In reality, it takes about two years for a widow to move on from distress. What could you do for her?

- Baby-sit for free so she can get some time to herself.
- Clean her house.
- Take care of the yard work.
- Shovel the snow.
- Provide things that she and her children need as well as financial support.
- Take her out for coffee and listen to her.
- Make sure she has a turkey for Thanksgiving and presents for Christmas.
- Invite her to your house to have dinner and hang out.
- You add to this list.

Visit prisoners in jail or teens in juvenile hall. You won't be able to bring them many presents, but you can spend some time with them and listen to what they are feeling. If God can forgive you, He can certainly forgive those in prison. You have a chance to share Jesus Christ with men and women that desperately need hope. I would recommend that men visit men and women visit women.

Spend time with those in nursing homes. My mother went into a very good nursing home, but it was still so depressing. It smelled bad and many of the older people were without hope. People have forgotten about them and some of them never have visitors. You will become a ray of sunshine in their lives. You are scared because you don't know what to talk about; ask them about what it was like when they were growing up. You will hear a lot of great stories. I believe that once you visit you will want to go back again. Maybe you could even adopt a grandparent and have them come to your house.

Go to a children's hospital or visit a cancer ward. Spend time with those that are very sick and may be dying. They are scared and need people that will listen and seek to understand them. These are people who are about to step into eternity and you will have a unique opportunity to tell them about Jesus.

Reach out to the lonely, depressed, and needy. They are at your school every day and are desperate for someone to love and care for them.

Why is this kind of ministry pure and faultless? Because you are doing it without expecting anything back in return. What can these people do for you? What can the widow or orphan really give to you? Nothing. You are doing this with no ulterior motives. You are looking to serve and to love these individuals.

Get out your Bible and read Matthew 20:20-28 and take special note of verses twenty-six to twenty-eight. If you want to be considered great in the Kingdom of God, then be a servant. Follow Christ's example. He didn't come to be served, but to serve and give His life as a ransom for many.

Romans 15:1-2 tells us we are to look after the weak and please our neighbor for his good, to build him up. As you are doing this important ministry to reach those in need, be sure that you are also keeping yourself from being polluted by the world. **It is hard to follow Jesus, but it is easy to love the world.** It is easy to become polluted by the world and to give into our cravings. John warns us in 1 John 2:15-17, *"Do not love the world or anything in the world. If anyone loves the world, the love of the Father is not in him. For everything in the world-the cravings of sinful man, the lust of the eyes and the boasting of what he has and does-comes not from the Father but from the world. The world and its desires pass away, but the man who does the will of God lives forever."*

Where will you invest your life? Will you invest in the things of the world or the things of God? Choose to invest your life in what will last. The things of the world, money, popularity, lust of the eyes, sinful cravings, stuff, and more stuff, will pass away, but the person that decides to invest their life in God and do what He asks will last forever.

Now get out there and be in the world, but not of the world. Impact the world and don't let the world impact you in a negative way. People are waiting for you to love them, will you answer the call?

## SOMETHING TO THINK ABOUT:

1. When was the last time you did ministry that was pure and faultless?

2. Part of service should be to get out of your comfort zone.

3. Do not love the world.

## SOMETHING TO PRAY ABOUT:

Ask God to lay on your heart someone or some group that you can minister to in a way that is pure and faultless. Ask Him to reveal to you anything that is polluting your life and tell Him that you will be willing to turn away from it.

## USE THIS SPACE TO JOURNAL ABOUT WHAT GOD IS SAYING TO YOU:

# DAY TWENTY-EIGHT – JAMES 2:1

## SOMETHING TO STUDY:

*"My brothers, as believers in our glorious Lord Jesus Christ, don't
show favoritism."*
James 2:1

An immature Christian can talk all about what they believe, but
a mature Christian lives out their faith. Age has little to do with
Christian maturity. I know seventeen year olds who are more spiritually
mature than some seventy year olds. One measuring stick for spiritual
maturity is how you treat other people. Every youth group has its
cliques and sometimes visitors find it hard to fit into the group. That is
a measure of spiritual maturity. A youth group that is mature is
sensitive and welcoming to those who are visiting.

It is always interesting to see how students respond to me when
I show up to speak. Some groups are immediately very kind, loving,
and accepting of me, while other groups treat me like I have a
contagious disease. Usually, by the end of the weekend, we are all great
friends. However, this is only because I have been walking around
reaching out to them. Someone new is not going to be aggressive in
reaching out to the group. They will stand in the corner and hope
someone will talk to them. The way a group treats me is usually the
way they treat others that come into their group.

When I was Director of Student Ministries, I knew we had
taken a huge step when we began to reach out to those who were
visitors and those that came across as different. One Wednesday night,
we had about two hundred teens packed into the room. Students were
playing foosball, pool, ping pong, and eating, but mostly talking. All of
a sudden, some guys walked into the room wearing occult t-shirts.
Their faces were painted white with black tear drops and black lips.
Before I could say anything, a bunch of students walked over to them
and began to welcome them and show them around. When that
happened, I knew we had taken a step toward spiritual maturity.

It is OK to have best friends, but not at the exclusion of
everyone else. Your relationships with your friends should never
resemble a circle, because if it does it means it is closed to others.
Instead your relationships should look like a horseshoe, you can hang

with your friends, but there is also an opening for others to join you and feel welcome.

What does it really mean to show favoritism? It means that you treat some people better than you treat others because of money they have, fame they posses, physical beauty you're attracted to, position they hold, or their amount of popularity. You are partial to these people because of what you think you can get out of the relationship.

This is being written to Christians. John refers to us as brothers and believers in our glorious Lord Jesus Christ. If there is one group of people that shouldn't be showing favoritism and judging others, it ought to be us as Christians. We all stand on equal ground before God Almighty. No one is any better than anyone else, we are all sinners saved by grace. Do you think that Jesus will like people better because they are a cheerleader or football player, or drive a BMW, or live in a big house, or always look good on the outside? NO! So shouldn't we follow in His footsteps? We need to treat others the way Jesus treats us.

Notice that Jesus Christ is glorious and when we stand before Him we are not thinking of the greatness or power of man, but we stand in awe of the Creator of the universe. Spend more time in God's presence and you will not be so impressed with man.

Check out Isaiah 40:15-17 and tell me, what does it say about man?

- The nations are like a drop in a bucket.
- They are regarded as dust on the scales.
- God weights the islands as though they were fine dust.
- Lebanon is not sufficient for altar fires.
- All the animals or Lebanon are not enough for burnt offerings.
- Before Him all the nations are as nothing.
- They are regarded as worthless and less than nothing.

In other words God is not impressed with all that we have accomplished on the outside. The heart has always been more important to Him. So don't spend your days looking up to man. Psalm 103:15-16 says, *"As for man, his days are like grass, he flourishes like a flower of the field; the wind blows over it and it is gone, and its place remembers it no more."*

Don't be impressed with man. Be impressed with God. Don't make some musician, movie star, or athlete your hero. **Make God your hero.** When you see others the way God does, then you won't be showing favoritism.

God is glorious and not man. Isaiah 6:1-4 says, *"In the year that King Uzziah died, I saw the Lord seated on a throne, high and exalted, and the train of his robe filled the temple. Above him were seraphs, each with six wings: With two wings they covered their faces; with two they covered their feet, and with two they were flying. And they were calling to one another: 'Holy, holy, holy is the Lord Almighty; the whole earth is full of his glory.' At the sound of their voices the doorposts and thresholds shook and the temple was filled with smoke."* Now that is impressive!

One day your twenty-fifth high school reunion will crack you up. All these people that you thought were so cool will be old and fat. The quarterback will be bald and suffering from furniture disease. That is when his chest falls into his drawers. You will say to yourself, "I can't believe that I used to look up to and be in awe of these people." I found most of the people at my reunion to be pretty sad individuals who had made a lot of bad choices. Some were working on their third and fourth marriages. But back in high school, they were shown a lot of favoritism because they were cute or could throw a football or got straight A's or had the lead in the musical.

So get a head start on your twenty-fifth reunion and stop showing favoritism. Respect man, but don't worship him. Be kind to man, but don't allow him to manipulate you. Have some good friends, but make sure that you are also including others that may need a friend.

## SOMETHING TO THINK ABOUT:

1. Do you show favoritism?

2. Kneeling before God will help you stand strong before man.

3. Are you showing spiritual maturity or immaturity? Is your youth ministry showing spiritual maturity or immaturity?

## SOMETHING TO PRAY ABOUT:

Ask God to help you see man the way He does. Ask Him to make you aware if you are showing any favoritism. Pray that He would lead you to individuals who are feeling left out.

## USE THIS SPACE TO JOURNAL ABOUT WHAT GOD IS SAYING TO YOU:

# DAY TWENTY-NINE – JAMES 2:2

## SOMETHING TO STUDY:

*"Suppose a man comes into your meeting wearing a gold ring and fine
clothes, and a poor man in shabby clothes also comes in."*
James 2:2

Who would your church prefer to see, someone dressed up or
someone that looks like a homeless person? How would people respond
to these two individuals? How would you respond? Would you find it
easier to approach the well-dressed person and talk to them? Would
you seek to avoid the homeless person?

We are quick to judge by how someone looks on the outside.
We jump to conclusions when we look at someone. They must be like
this, act like this, or feel like this because of how we perceive them.
Nine times out of ten our first impressions are totally wrong.

In youth ministry, (you often find two groups) we are always
separating the haves and the have-nots. There is the in-group and those
left on the outside. The in-group looks down on the outsiders and the
outsider's gossip about the in-group. What is the result? We have a
youth group that is divided and all the little cliques are fighting among
each other. How do you bring a non-Christian into that setting? How
accepted and loved will they feel? How unified does the youth group
appear? The answers are: you don't, they won't, and not at all.

Stop showing favoritism and begin to treat all people as equal.
You miss out on a lot of great friendships because you judge people
based on the outside. You think they are too fat, ugly, socially awkward,
uncoordinated, gross, out of style, or just pathetic! Is that right or
wrong? I will give you a hint…it is wrong!

**We must come together as the Body of Christ and start
caring about one another so that the world sees a difference.** Teens
at your school attack and tear others down, but your youth group ought
to be different. Students should be able to show up and feel like they
are accepted, understood, and loved. This will only happen if you start
to make changes and take the steps to tear down the walls. What is
stopping you from taking that stand and speaking out for unity? I know

your Youth Pastor wants that to happen, but it won't happen until teenagers own their youth group and begin to live out their faith.

I want you to start the process of unifying your youth group and reaching out to those who are different from you. Talk to your Youth Pastor about your heart and desire to see things change.

## SOMETHING TO THINK ABOUT:

1. Are you one that judges others by what they look like on the outside?

2. The world has the right to judge us as Christians by whether we are unified or      not.
3. Is your youth group unified or filled with cliques? What are you doing to make a difference?

## SOMETHING TO PRAY ABOUT:

Ask God if you judge people. Ask Him to give you a love for the unlovely and tell Him that you are willing to be used by Him to reach out to others who are not a part of your group. Ask Him to break down the walls in your youth ministry.

## USE THIS SPACE TO JOURNAL ABOUT WHAT GOD IS SAYING TO YOU:

# DAY THIRTY – JAMES 2:3-4

## SOMETHING TO STUDY:

*"If you show special attention to the man wearing fine clothes and say, 'Here's a good seat for you,' but say to the poor man, 'You stand there' or 'Sit on the floor by my feet,' have you not discriminated among yourselves and become judges with evil thoughts?"*
James 2:3-4

Here are two individuals, a rich man and a homeless man again, and right away the church shows the one wearing the fine clothes special treatment while the homeless person can stand or sit on the floor. Do you see anything wrong with this whole situation?

James is showing us two extremes, a person that is wealthy with fine clothes and a gold ring and someone who is very poor. He uses these two extremes to show us that if favoritism is wrong in this case, then it is wrong in every case.

Let me make some observations about favoritism:

- How rich was Jesus? How popular was He? How much stuff did He own? If you reject the poor, then you reject Jesus.

- When we say poor, we are talking about more than just money. I know some of you are thinking that you wouldn't reject a homeless person. But we are also talking about being poor in looks, style, social graces, tact, abilities, hygiene, grades, etc. How do you respond to a person that smells or is rude? To show favoritism because someone doesn't meet our expectations of what we think they should be like is wrong.

- When you show favoritism, you set yourself up as a judge and there is only one judge and that is God. We are not the ones to decide who is acceptable to God and who isn't. The poor should be the very people that we are reaching out to. Read Psalm 82:3, *"Defend the cause of the weak and fatherless; maintain the rights of the poor and oppressed."*

- The favoritism you show reveals that you have evil thoughts. You favor these people because you have ulterior motives. You are thinking about what you can get out of the relationship. You don't like a poor person because they can't really do anything for you. You don't really care about the person you only care about what the person can do for you. So the money, appearance, popularity, car, etc. is more important than the person and that is just wrong.

- It is not wrong to be rich and wealthy. Those people need Jesus just as much as poor people do. So let's not make the mistake of showing favoritism to the poor over the rich.

**We should treat all individuals with the same respect and honor.** We all need Jesus and we are all just passing through this world.

## SOMETHING TO THINK ABOUT:

1. How many poor people do you reach out to?

2. To show favoritism is to reveal that you have evil thoughts.

3. Treat others the way Jesus treats you.

## SOMETHING TO PRAY ABOUT:

Ask God to open your eyes to the poor that are around you every day. Ask Him to give you ideas of ways that you can reach out to them.

## USE THIS SPACE TO JOURNAL ABOUT WHAT GOD IS SAYING TO YOU:

# DAY THIRTY-ONE – JAMES 2:5

## SOMETHING TO STUDY:

*"Listen, my dear brothers: Has not God chosen those who are poor in the eyes of the world to be rich in faith and to inherit the kingdom he promised those who love him?"*
James 2:5

God has chosen the poor to be rich in faith and inherit the kingdom of God. So if you reject the poor, you reject the very people God has chosen. Does that make sense to you?

The poor see their need more than the rich. The poor understand that they need help and are willing to humble themselves. The rich tend to think that they can do it themselves. They think they don't need anyone and that includes God.

Check out 1 Corinthians 1:26-29. Read it and then I will hit on some of the highlights. What does it say about those who came to Christ? Not many were wise, not many were influential, and not many were of noble birth. Instead, God chose the foolish, weak, lowly, and despised things. Here are a couple of thoughts.

- Even though many of those who came to Christ were not wise, influential, or of noble birth, some were. God sees all people the same and desires that all people would come to Him.
- God does choose the foolish, weak, lowly, and despised. This list pretty much describes Greg Speck. These are the people that see their need and respond to the Holy Spirit's prompting. It is easier for these people to humble themselves. Sometimes the wise, influential, and noble can struggle with pride. Is that a problem? Yes, because of what Proverbs 3:34 says, *"...God opposes the proud but gives grace to the humble."* Never place yourself in a position of opposition to God. That is a battle you will not win.

Why does the church favor the rich? Because the church can be very greedy. Just think of all the great things we could have if we had more money. We could have our own yacht or musical toilets that play "Just as I Am" while you sit on them. Does God need man's money?

No. He has access to all money. We don't need rich people in our church, we just need to be faithful to do what God is calling us to do.

Part of what God is calling us to do is reach out to the poor. Feed and clothe the homeless, care for those who are struggling emotionally, and love the unlovely. Everyone needs Jesus, the high and the lowly, the happy and the sad, the rich and the poor.

I pray and ask God to reveal to the rich just how poor they really are and how much they need Jesus. Wealth becomes a mask that covers over what is really important and keeps the rich from taking the steps needed to grow as men and women.

You are the church of the future and you are the church of today. So make sure you are headed in the right direction with the right priorities. **Bring Jesus to a world that desperately needs to know Him.**

## SOMETHING TO THINK ABOUT:

1. All the stuff in the world doesn't impress God and it shouldn't impress us.

2. Are you willing to be poor in the eyes of the world?

3. Are you humbling yourself before the Lord?

## SOMETHING TO PRAY ABOUT:

Ask God to give you a longing for the things that mean something to Him. Not money and materials, but things such as humility, a soft heart, strength of character, deep love, faithfulness, and a gentle and quiet spirit.

## USE THIS SPACE TO JOURNAL ABOUT WHAT GOD IS SAYING TO YOU:

# DAY THIRTY-TWO – JAMES 2:6a

## SOMETHING TO STUDY:

*"But you have insulted the poor..."*
James 2:6a

When you show favoritism toward the rich, you have revealed a terrible attitude. You insult the poor and cause them to feel ashamed, dishonored, and humiliated. Think about it . . . Does a poor person have feelings? Do they struggle emotionally? If you grew up in the same circumstances and had the same problems, might you be just like them? Be sensitive to those who are poor.

How hurt do you feel when someone discriminates against you? Everyone is hanging out on a Saturday except you, everyone is invited to a party but not you, all are going to the movies but they don't tell you about it. There is a pain you feel deep down in your heart when you are discriminated against. You feel unwelcome and of little value or worth. It impacts your self-worth and you start to feel really bad about yourself. The poor feel the same way when you insult them.

**We are to live as Christ lived and to love as Christ loved.** This means we are reaching out to the poor and lowly of the world. Read Matthew 11:4-5 and see how Jesus ministered to the poor of His day.

The blind received sight.
The lame walked.
The leper was cured.
The deaf heard.
The dead were raised.
Good news was preached to the poor.

The blind, leper, lame, deaf, and poor were the losers of Jesus' day. They were totally rejected by others and even by their own families. But Jesus sets the example for us by reaching out to these people. Who are the rejects today at your school? How about the fat, awkward, smart, poor, socially awkward, uncoordinated, and style challenged. Are you reaching out to these people? Do you sit with them at lunch time? Do you invite them to your house? Do you hang out with them? By spending time with them you are saying that they are someone of worth and value. You set them free from the bondage of self-hate.

You are called to love those the world has rejected. Reach out to them and you will be giving them hope and a sense of purpose. God will use you and the spiritually blind will receive sight, the emotionally lame will walk, the self-hate leper will be cured, the deaf to the truth will hear, the dead to hope will be raised, and the good news will be preached to the poor. In other words, God will be using you to make a difference in your world. Take the steps you need to take and do what needs to be done.

## SOMETHING TO THINK ABOUT:

1. Have you ever been left out? How did it make you feel?

2. Have you considered having lunch with someone outside your group?

3. When you care for the poor, you are caring for Jesus.

## SOMETHING TO PRAY ABOUT:

Ask God to give you His eyes to see the poor at your school and in your neighborhood. Ask Him to give you the courage and the words to say as you reach out to these people.

## USE THIS SPACE TO JOURNAL ABOUT WHAT GOD IS SAYING TO YOU:

# DAY THIRTY-THREE – JAMES 2:6b-7

## SOMETHING TO STUDY:

*"... Is it not the rich who are exploiting you? Are they not the ones who are dragging you into court? Are they not the ones who are slandering the noble name of him to whom you belong?"*
James 2:6b-7

You show favoritism to the rich, give them the best seat, give them special attention, and seek to meet their needs. So how do they repay all this attention and kindness? They exploit you, drag you into court, and slander God's name.

Congratulations on your very bad choice to honor the rich and neglect the poor. **James is saying that the rich are causing you the majority of your problems and not the poor.**

Why is it the rich person who drags you into court is causing all these hassles? Because they feel entitled and believe that people ought to give them special attention. They have become accustomed to people doing things the way they want them done. If you don't meet their expectations, they get upset and may even drag you into court.

During the summers, I used to take teens overseas on short-term missions trips. On our flight home, I was talking to one of the airline people and I ask them, "Are teenagers pretty much the same around the world?" She said, "No, Australian teens are pretty laid back, French teens are out of control, and American teens are very demanding." Yep, we Americans have a lot of money so we think we are entitled to a high degree of service and we demand it.

Many rich people do this; they demand that things be done their way. Is that true of all rich? No, there are amazing servants of God that humble themselves, love the poor, show the fruit of the Spirit, and at the same time are very wealthy.

But the rich who do not humble themselves are attacking the church in three ways:

- They exploit the church and use it to get what they want. The rich have an agenda and there are certain things they like and certain things they don't like. So, they will do whatever it takes to: have the kind of music they like played on Sunday morning, have the kind of Youth Pastor they want, have the kind of programs they enjoy, and support the kind of ministry or charity that is important to them.

- They take the church to court. If they don't get what they want or think that the church is not using their money correctly, they sue the church. They are like spoiled little children who take their football and go home because they aren't winning. But instead of going home, they go to court.

- They slander the name of God. How do they slander God's name? By denying Him or the truth of His Word, rejecting Him, making fun of Him, using His name as a swear word, or degrading Him.

Why would the church show favoritism toward these people over the poor? It is crazy, but you see it happening all the time. Don't fall into the same trap!

## SOMETHING TO THINK ABOUT:

1. Who is more likely to persecute you: the popular or the unpopular?

2. Do you ever favor the rich over the poor?

3. Are you demanding?

## SOMETHING TO PRAY ABOUT:

Ask God to give you the opportunity and boldness to speak truth to your church.

## USE THIS SPACE TO JOURNAL ABOUT WHAT GOD IS SAYING TO YOU:

# DAY THIRTY-FOUR – JAMES 2:8

## SOMETHING TO STUDY:

*"If you really keep the royal law found in Scripture, 'Love your neighbor as yourself,' you are doing right."*
James 2:8

D.L. Moody said, "Every Bible should be bound in shoe leather!" What he meant is that we need to practice what we preach. The Word is from the very mouth of God and needs to be made practical in our lives. One way to do that is to love your neighbor as yourself. Your neighbor is anyone you meet who needs help. It is not a matter of geography, but of opportunity. It includes the person at school, your neighborhood, church, the mall, the place you work, the health club, the swimming pool, the movies, the restroom…maybe you should wait until they get out of the restroom.

**Love is practical and it meets the needs of the person that you have come in contact with.** The other day a guy came into my office (Starbucks) and asked if I had any spare change. He said that he wanted to buy some food. I don't give out money because it could end up being used to buy alcohol or drugs. Instead, I said, "I won't give you money, but I will buy you some food." So I bought the man something to eat and drink. If you are willing to love those around you, then the Lord will set up divine appointments and bring people into your life so you can show them love. That is the main responsibility of a Christian: To love God first and foremost and then to love others.

Why is it called the royal law? Let me suggest two reasons.

- It comes from the King. God is the one who has passed that law down to us and He is the King of King's. That makes it royal!
- It is part of the greatest commandment. Read Matthew 22:34-40 and let me hit on some of the highlights. An expert of the law asks Jesus what is the greatest commandment. Jesus replies that loving God is number one, but the second greatest is to love your neighbor. Then He tells him that all the law and the prophets hang on these two commandments.

There are five practical ways that you can love your neighbor. Gary Chapman has written 7,347 books on the love languages. Like love languages for husbands, wives, parents, children, teenagers, small dogs, and sea creatures. OK, just kidding, he hasn't written that many books, but he has written a lot and that is how I first learned about love languages. So here are the five ways you can love your neighbor.

- Words

You are going to seek to build them up. It is very easy to be sarcastic and attacking because you can hide behind walls. Your excuse is always, "I was just kidding, come on can't you take a joke." But if we are going to truly love someone, we must be willing to take a risk and verbally build them up. A kind word is like a breath of fresh air or a cup of cold water on a hot day. It brings life and encouragement, hope and respect, joy and dignity. Try saying something nice to someone God has brought across your path. Find something to appreciate and admire. Don't just focus on the physical. Try to catch them being good. Look for an act of service or kindness and then acknowledge it.

I was at my bank checking out my millions of dollars when I heard one of the assistants helping an older couple that was very confused. She was so patient and explained everything several times until they understood. Before I left, I stopped at her desk and told her how impressed I was with the way she had helped the couple.

It is fun to catch people doing things well and then compliment them: someone picking up litter, sweeping a floor, or being kind to a person or animal, a waitress or waiter that is really good, a child behaving well, or anything that God shows you. Giving people a word of encouragement can make their day, week, and even month!

- Time

Taking the time to listen shows someone that they are of worth and value. Ask someone how they are doing and really mean it. Go out with someone just for the purpose of listening to them. Sometimes we think that we need to have all the answers and we don't. Most people don't want you to fix anything, they just want you to care. People are desperate for someone who will listen and care about them and all of us as Christians are called to do those two things.

I am so thankful to God that He allows me to travel around the world speaking to teenagers. I love the speaking, but I also love spending time with individual students and listening to them. That is just as important as speaking and in some cases even more important. Listening allows me to minister to specific needs plus it keeps me on the cutting edge of understanding teens and what is happening in their lives.

- Touch

Put your arm around someone, shake their hand, give them a high five, or pound it. Sometimes when I give teens a chance to come to the alter, I will say, "Some of you need a 'Dad hug' and I am available to give that to you." I will have so many teens come to me for a hug and many will be guys. Most everyone desires and welcomes the warmth of human touch. Some of us are huggers and some are not. But even if you are uncomfortable hugging, you can still touch someone in purity.

- Service

Here you are looking for ways to show God's love in practical ways. When you serve someone you are saying, "I want to make your load lighter." What can you do to serve the people around you? Here is what I say to teens, "Always leave a place looking better than when you arrived." I will pick up in a restroom, if the coffee station with the sugar and milk is messy I will clean it up, I pick up litter and open doors for people, when I fly I pull things down from the overhead for other people. What can you do? The only thing that limits you is your creativity. You are looking to do random acts of kindness.

- Gifts

When you give someone a gift you are saying I am thinking about you when we are apart or I care enough to want to meet your needs. A gift could be anything: a note, can of coke, flower, candy bar, meal, etc. What could you give to someone that they would appreciate?

I want you to put the royal law into action and begin to love your neighbor. Your neighbor is the person that God brings into your life even if it's just for a moment.

## SOMETHING TO THINK ABOUT:

1. Every person that God brings into your life is your neighbor.

2. Are you practicing the love languages?

3. Be careful when you are showing love to a member of the opposite sex. It can send messages that you never meant to send, like you are interested in them romantically.

## SOMETHING TO PRAY ABOUT:

Ask God to make you a lover in the purest sense of the word. Ask Him to make you sensitive to those around you so that you can show them love. Pray for creativity in the different ways you can love others.

## USE THIS SPACE TO JOURNAL ABOUT WHAT GOD IS SAYING TO YOU:

# DAY THIRTY-FIVE – JAMES 2:9

## SOMETHING TO STUDY:

*"But if you show favoritism, you sin and are convicted by the law as*
*lawbreakers."*
James 2:9

Not only is favoritism wrong, it is also a sin. It's one thing to do something you shouldn't do, but it's another thing to sin. For example, I am on a diet and I shouldn't eat a chocolate chip cookie, but I do it anyway. This is not a wise choice, but it is not a sin. On the other hand, if your mom says, "Don't eat those chocolate chip cookies," and you tell her to kiss off and then eat them anyway, that is a sin. James is saying that showing favoritism is not only wrong, but it is also a sin. Now that is something that I definitely need to avoid.

Sin is a terrible thing and not to be taken lightly. How bad is sin? It killed Jesus Christ! He didn't have to go to the cross, but He did because of your sin and mine. I have heard teens say to me, "God understands when we sin because we are only human. He forgives me so it doesn't really matter if I sin as long as I repent." God does not tolerate, accept, or excuse sin. Yes, He will forgive you when you repent, but repenting means that you then turn from the sin. Don't ever fall into cheap grace that says, "I can go out and sin Monday through Saturday and then receive forgiveness on Sunday because I know that God loves me no matter what." That is wrong and you are taking advantage of God's grace.

We love to compare abilities, looks, style, and sometimes, even sin. Sometimes, when we are aware of sin in our lives, we excuse it because it isn't as bad as this other sin. "OK, I know that I have this clique and I exclude other people, but at least I am not murdering, stealing, robbing, etc." Sin is sin and God doesn't see degrees of sin. If He is calling you to get rid of a sin, then do it now! Satan will do anything to get a foothold in your life. If the first step is for you to show favoritism, then he is happy to help you take that step. His desire is to get you involved in sin one step at a time. After the sin of favoritism, he will add another sin like gossip and after that perhaps profanity. Next he suggests rebellion toward your parents and after that he wants you to start having sex. How did you get from showing favoritism and running around in your little group to sleeping with your boy/girlfriend? Satan patiently leads you one step and one sin at a time.

**Get rid of all sin in your life no matter how small or insignificant you think it to be.** What will you do when a voice whispers in your ear and says, "This sin isn't so bad, it's not that big of a deal." Whose voice do you think that is, God or the enemy? If you are listening to the enemy, you are now on very thin ice. Stop showing favoritism and stop it now. It is sin and sin needs to be avoided at all cost.

## SOMETHING TO THINK ABOUT:

1. You must hate sin because it killed Jesus and it can kill you.

2. Do you ever compare your sin to other sin and decide that is isn't that bad?

3. Have you ever fallen into cheap grace?

## SOMETHING TO PRAY ABOUT:

Ask God to keep you from sin and to convict you of any sin that you are holding onto in your life. Tell Him that you are willing to deal with all your sins, no matter how small you have thought the sin to be.

## USE THIS SPACE TO JOURNAL ABOUT WHAT GOD IS SAYING TO YOU:

# DAY THIRTY-SIX – JAMES 2:10-11

## SOMETHING TO STUDY:

*"For whoever keeps the whole law and yet stumbles at just one point is guilty of breaking all of it. For he who said, 'Do not commit adultery,' also said, 'Do not murder.' If you do not commit adultery but do commit murder, you have become a lawbreaker."*
James 2:10-11

Are you telling me that if I mess up in one area of the law that I have broken the whole law? How can that be? The law gives us direction for life. It also give us a goal of living that life to please God. When we break one law, we have moved off the path and we fall short of the goal. **Miss it by a foot or miss it by a mile, you have still missed the mark and that is not good enough.**

Imagine that you have two people who are going to jump a chasm that is one mile wide. One is an Olympic jumper and the other is totally uncoordinated. It really doesn't matter if one can jump a world record distance or if one falls off the edge, both men are dead. To only break one law or to break all the laws is the same, you have missed the goal that God has set up and you are headed for eternal death.

What is the law? Check out Exodus 20:1-17, what is this called? It is called the Ten Commandments (not the Ten Suggestions). This is the law and if you can keep the whole law, you can go to heaven. But this is not a multiple-choice test where you can choose the three that you like best, obey them, and ignore the rest. You must keep all of them and if you break one then you have broken the law. As you read the list, tell me how you are doing in keeping the whole law?

- Put no god's before the Lord God Almighty.
- Do not make for yourself an idol to worship.
- Do not take the Lord's name in vain.
- Remember the Sabbath and keep it holy.
- Honor your father and mother.
- Do not murder.
- Do not commit adultery.
- Do not steal.
- Do not give false testimony.

- Do not covet from your neighbor.

You might say to me, "I am a little shaky on honoring my father and mother and I may have used the Lord's name in vain, once, when I was really mad, but other than that I am doing fine." Really? Come on a journey of discovery with me.

Have you ever committed adultery? Maybe you would say, "No, that is one area that I have not fallen in at all." Take your Bible and turn to Matthew 5:27-28 and read about adultery. If you look at a woman lustfully, you have already committed adultery in your heart. This also applies to you women who lust after a guy thinking "He is so fine!" Now have you ever committed adultery? Most of would have to say…yes.

What about murder? Have you ever murdered anyone? You would say, "OK, I can see how I fell in the adultery area, but I am sure that I have never murdered anyone."

Turn in your Bible to Matthew 5:21-22. If you murder, then you are subject to judgment. But now it also says that if you are angry with your brother, you are subject to judgment. So being angry with your brother will bring judgment just like murder. Ever been angry with someone? Me too, so we are all in big trouble.

Listen to what God says to us in Matthew 5:20, *"For I tell you that unless your righteousness surpasses that of the Pharisees and the teachers of the law, you will certainly not enter the kingdom of heaven."* I want to make sure that you catch what is being said here. If you want to go to heaven, you better keep the whole law and if you break just one law, then you have broken all of the law and you are going to hell. Your righteousness must surpass the Pharisees and the teachers of the law or you are not getting into heaven. So how many of us will be going to heaven? Not me and I will go out on a limb and say not you either.

Go back to James 2:8 and see again the importance of the royal law. The Ten Commandments can be summed up in the royal law. Read Galatians 5:14, *"The entire law is summed up in a single command: 'Love your neighbor as yourself'."* If you show favoritism, you are no longer loving your neighbor as yourself, so you have broken the law of God. This is why it is so important to treat others with respect and honor and to make sure you are not excluding, being cruel to, or favoring others because of what you think you can get out of the relationship.

We are all falling short, not meeting God's standards and wandering away from His goal for our lives. We are all headed to hell because we have broken the royal law and in doing that we have broken all of the law. So what is the answer? What do I need to do? You need to be thankful for Christmas and Easter and everything they mean.

God looked down and saw that you and I had fallen short of the goal. He knew that we were law breakers that we're bound for hell. So He sent His only Son, Jesus Christ, to earth. That is a historical fact. He lived, breathed, and walked this earth. He brought the truth and showed us the way to God the Father. When the Pharisees and teachers of the law compared themselves to Jesus, they looked very bad. So they had a choice, they could change their lives or crucify Jesus. It is always easier to crucify someone else, so they killed Jesus and on the cross He took your sins. He as buried and three days later He rose from the grave, but your sins stayed buried. So even though we are law breakers, if we come to Jesus Christ, He will forgive our sins and open the door for us to live in heaven forever. That is why we so desperately need Jesus, because all of us are law-breakers.

James wants you to know how bad favoritism is impacting you and others. He wants you to get rid of this and live a life that brings a smile to God's face. When is the last time you set out to live a day to bring a smile to God's face? Well, today would be a great day to start.

## SOMETHING TO THINK ABOUT:

1. How important is it to keep the law? How well are you doing?

2. Do your friends know about the law and requirements for heaven?

3. How have you been doing when it comes to including others and not showing favoritism?

## SOMETHING TO PRAY ABOUT:

Thank Jesus that He came to pay the price for your sins. Thank Him for loving you even though you are a law breaker. Thank Him that one day you will live forever in heaven with Him.

## USE THIS SPACE TO JOURNAL ABOUT WHAT GOD IS SAYING TO YOU:

# DAY THIRTY-SEVEN – JAMES 2:12

## SOMETHING TO STUDY:

*"Speak and act as those who are going to be judged by the law that gives freedom..."*
James 2:12

James is talking to us about two areas in which we will be judged. First of all, our words will be judged. What we say and how we say it is important to God. Since we are going to be judged in this area, it makes sense that we think before we speak. What does Matthew 12:36 say to you? *"But I tell you that men will have to give account on the day of judgment for every careless word they have spoken."* That should get our attention and give us pause. These are not just careless words that we speak in front of others, but these are words that we utter when no one else is around. Like when the jerk driving the car in front of you, who doesn't have a clue, and should have his license revoked because he is sharing a brain with someone else and today is not his day to have the brain and you want...Oops, I think I got carried away. There have been times I have uttered things in my car that I wouldn't want anyone else to hear. But then it hits me, God is hearing everything that I am saying.

Let me take it a step further. What about the words that we think? Are those a problem? Yes, because God says that out of the overflow of your heart you speak. The good man brings up the good that is stored in his heart and the evil man brings up the bad that dwells in his heart (Matthew 12:33-35). The words you are thinking are an indication of what you are putting into your mind. For whatever you put into your mind goes into your heart and from your heart you speak. Plus, if you are thinking these things, it will just be a matter of time before you start to speak them.

How you say something is also important. You can either make it is easy for someone to receive what you say or you can make it hard. Every time you communicate a message it is made up of three parts: 7% is the words you use, 38% is your voice inflection, volume, and how you say it, and 55% of every message you communicate is non-verbal-- how you stand, your facial expression, what you do with your hands, etc. So, I stand with my hands on my hips, a scowl on my face, and in a loud voice say, "I am not upset!" 7% of the message says that I am not upset, but 93% says I am really upset.

What is easier for you to accept, "You are never around anymore" or "I miss you?" What sounds better, "You are a terrible driver" or "When I ride with you it makes me glad that I know Jesus?" How you say something is important because it will make it either easy or difficult for others to accept the message.

Secondly, we are going to be judged by our actions. Here is what we read in Colossians 3:23-24, *"Whatever you do, work at it with all your heart, as working for the Lord, not for men, since you know that you will receive an inheritance from the Lord as a reward. It is the Lord Christ you are serving."*

**You belong to Jesus Christ and your service belongs to Him.** So no matter what you are doing, you are doing it for the Lord. This means that we should be doing everything with excellence. Some people work really hard when someone else is around, but then they slow way down when no one is looking. For us as Christians, we realize that someone is always watching so we want to make sure that the King is pleased with our work.

I think back on how hard I worked in football to impress the coach so that I would make the starting lineup. When he was looking, I would kill myself just to hear him say, "Good job, Speck." How much harder should I be serving my Lord and Savior Jesus Christ? One day I want to hear Him say to me, "Welcome, good and faithful servant."

If God can trust you to work really hard and represent Him well when no one is around, then He can trust you to represent Him well when others can see. It is God who will give you favor, it is God who will open the door for you to get a good job, it is God who will meet your needs and take care of you. You must decide that you will do the job well because you are working for the Lord.

As I work on this book, a Christian who is a realtor came and sat behind me. She was talking to one of her clients. He wanted her to come and see a home that another realtor was showing him and get her opinion. The realtor said, "I will take off my wedding ring and you can tell him that I am your girlfriend and then I can see the house and tell you what I think." As they were leaving, they stopped at my table

107

because the realtor's child and my child went to the same high school. She gave me her card and said, "If you ever want to buy or sell a house let me know." When she left, I threw her card away. Her words and actions told me that she couldn't be trusted. If she is willing to be deceptive and lie to another realtor, then she is capable of deceiving and lying to me.

One big area that will allow you to work for God is school. I know this might not be your favorite place to go or your favorite thing to do, but it is a big part of your life right now and it is a lot of time for you to waste. You need to change your attitude when it comes to academics. There are three areas in which you can serve God when it comes to school.

- Academics: This is a preparation period for you and your goal is to learn all you can so that you can be the best possible individual for the Lord to work through. So study hard and learn the material not to get a grade or class ranking, but for the glory of God.

- Teachers: Contrary to popular belief your teachers are human. They also need Jesus. You must be that example in class by paying attention, appreciating them, and working hard. Your lifestyle in class will either draw your teachers toward Christ or push them further away.

- Peers: Your friends need to see the reality of Jesus Christ in your life. If you are making sure that your actions are pleasing to God, you will impact your friends in a positive way.

Words and actions are important to God and they should be important to us, because one day we will be judged on what we have said and how we have acted.

## SOMETHING TO THINK ABOUT:

1. What have your words been like this past week?

2. How has your attitude been toward school? What changes do you need to make?

3. You aren't ready to die for Jesus until you are ready to live for Jesus.

**SOMETHING TO PRAY ABOUT:**

Pray that the words of your mouth and your actions might be pleasing and honoring to the Lord. Ask Him to make you conscious of the words that are going to come out of your mouth before you say them. Tell Him that you want to work for Him today.

**USE THIS SPACE TO JOURNAL ABOUT WHAT GOD IS SAYING TO YOU:**

# DAY THIRTY-EIGHT – JAMES 2:13

## SOMETHING TO STUDY:

*"...because judgment without mercy will be shown to anyone who has not been merciful. Mercy triumphs over judgment."*
James 2:13

Thank goodness for this statement. If judgment triumphed over mercy, we would be in big trouble. How would we stand up to God's judgment? The answer is we wouldn't. But God shows us mercy so that we can pass that on to others. I have said it before and I will probably say it again, we need to treat people the way Jesus treats us. God is saying that He will be happy to treat you the way you treat others. Do you want to be judged, then start to judge others. Do you want to be treated with mercy, then show mercy to others.

It is easy for me to think of legalistic schools and churches and how they are so critical of others, especially those in the body of Christ. They make up their lists of dos and don'ts. Anyone that doesn't abide by their list is now under their judgment. I would send my children to a secular university before I would send them to one of those legalistic schools or churches.

But then God says, "What about you Greg? What about the times that you judge others and are critical of others, like those in legalistic churches?" It is so easy to point a finger at someone else and turn a blind eye toward myself. The person that needs to change the most when it comes to judging and being critical is me and maybe you.

This does not mean that we should ignore sin or candy-coat it. No, we need to speak out against sin. God has set before us the truth in His Word. No amount of legislature or media changes the truth. We never compromise God's Word and we speak out against sin but at the same time we love and show mercy toward others.

**Both mercy and justice come from God.** When we turn to Him in repentance, humility, and faith, we will find mercy. When we live in sin and unbelief, we will experience God's justice. Think of people who have gotten away with crimes, sometimes even murder. Have they really gotten away with their sin? No, God is a just God and one day they will have to stand before Him and discover His justice. Better to face the justice of man, rather than the justice of the Lord.

It is easy to be critical, but it takes work and practice to show mercy. It is easy to see the things that we don't like, but it takes effort to see the positive in others. Starting now, show others the mercy you want to experience from Jesus Christ.

## SOMETHING TO THINK ABOUT:

1. Have you been showing others mercy?

2. How has God been treating you?

3. Would you rather have mercy or justice from God?

## SOMETHING TO PRAY ABOUT:

Ask God to give you a compassion for others around you. Tell him that you want to treat people with mercy and kindness. Ask Him to point out when you're being judgmental.

## USE THIS SPACE TO JOURNAL ABOUT WHAT GOD IS SAYING TO YOU:

# DAY THIRTY-NINE – JAMES 2:14

## SOMETHING TO STUDY:

*"What good is it, my brothers, if a man claims to have faith but has no deeds? Can such faith save him?"*
James 2:14

James is targeting the person that says he is a Christian but there is no evidence in the way he lives. This person substitutes words for deeds--they know all the right words, they can answer all the biblical questions, they can quote verses, their prayers are theologically sound, and they can even share a word of testimony. But if you watch their lifestyle, you see no evidence of a love or commitment to Jesus Christ. They think that words are enough, but they are completely wrong.

James asks you two really important questions. Can a man have faith in Jesus Christ and not live for Jesus Christ? And can that kind of faith save him? First of all, I believe that salvation is from Christ and we do not work for it or earn it. It is a gift of God and not a result of works. But once I have come to Christ and experienced His grace, shouldn't I be living for Him? Shouldn't I want to live for Him? And if I don't live for Him, what does that say about my relationship with Him?

You tell me that you are a football player, but you never go to practice and you never show up for a game. So are you really a football player? I would say no. You tell me you are a baker, but you never bake anything and you don't go into a kitchen, but you know a lot about baking. Are you really a baker? I would say no. You tell me that you are a Christian, but you never live for Jesus and you're involved in willful sin. Are you really a Christian? I would say no. Look, God knows who is and isn't a Christian. He knows who has really asked Him into their heart and who hasn't. But I would hate to base my eternity on the fact that I asked Jesus into my heart when I was three years old and have never really lived for Him.

**Just because you claim to have faith doesn't mean you really have faith.** I can claim to be the President of the United States, but the fact is that I am not the president. If I claim to love my wife, but never show her I love her, what does that say about my love? It says it is empty and without foundation because if I really loved Bonnie then I would show her. Not only that, but it would be a pleasure to show her and be something that I would want to do.

Do you love Jesus Christ? Then you would want to live for Him. You would want other people to see that love. It would be a pleasure and privilege to follow Him and not a burden.

## SOMETHING TO THINK ABOUT:

1. If you were arrested for being a Christian would there be enough evidence to convict you? Would people in your school be shocked to find out that you claim to be a Christian?

2. If you love Jesus, then live for Jesus!

3. If your actions do not back up your words, then your words are worthless.

## SOMETHING TO PRAY ABOUT:

Tell Christ that you want to live for Him. Ask Him what He wants you to do and tell Him that you will be obedient.

## USE THIS SPACE TO JOURNAL ABOUT WHAT GOD IS SAYING TO YOU:

# DAY FORTY – JAMES 2:15-16

## SOMETHING TO STUDY:

*"Suppose a brother or sister is without clothes and daily food. If one of you says to him, 'Go, I wish you well; keep warm and well fed', but does nothing about his physical needs, what good is it?"*
James 2:15-16

Good intentions are not good enough. You can have a lot of great plans to do all kinds of wonderful things for the cause of Christ, but if you don't follow up on these plans with action, then it is all empty.

You have probably gone to retreats and been a part of missions trips and you probably made commitments about what you were going to do when you got home. Did you actually follow through and do those things? What good is it to see the needs before you and not do anything about it?

James' illustration here is especially sad because it involves someone of whom you are aware. You know what their needs are and you even communicate with them what they would long for, but you do nothing to help them. Where is your faith? Where is your love for Jesus Christ? Explain to me how you can claim to be a Christian, but then ignore something so in your face as a brother or sister without clothes or daily food?

Don't we do this every day? We see the needs around us and we have become cold and callous to those needs. It is someone else's problem, but not my problem. Let the homeless shelter give them food and clothing. I have homework, friends to hang out with, stuff to buy for me, practice, work, and other things more important than the needs of those around me. Do you know how I know that the suffering is not important to you? Because you don't do anything about it and your actions or lack of actions speak very loudly about what you are like on the inside.

The big cry today is hypocrisy because we see Christians that claim one thing and practice another. How about a Christian that believes something, but does nothing? Are they being hypocritical? **You must live out your faith through your actions.** Read Matthew

114

5:16, "In the same way, let your light shine before men, that they may see your good deeds and praise your Father in heaven." You shine your light before others by doing something. People must see your good deeds, your faith in action, and your desire to meet the needs of those around you.

If you are willing to help others, then God will bring people across your path who you can care about. It will cost you time, effort, and money. A real faith sees what the needs are and then steps out to meet those needs. Get your focus off yourself and see what is going on around you.

## SOMETHING TO THINK ABOUT:

1. What are some of the needs around you? Now step out and do something.

2. Your faith is worthless and useless if it is not accompanied by good deeds.

3. To know what is right to do and not do it is sin.

## SOMETHING TO PRAY ABOUT:

Ask God to make you aware of the needs around you and to give you the courage to step out and do something about it.

## USE THIS SPACE TO JOURNAL ABOUT WHAT GOD IS SAYING TO YOU:

# DAY FORTY-ONE – JAMES 2:17

## SOMETHING TO STUDY:

*"In the same way, faith by itself, if it is not accompanied by action, is dead."*
James 2:17

We are not talking about saving faith because you are saved by faith alone and you can't add anything to what Jesus Christ has done for you. His death on the cross is all you need to step into a personal relationship with Him. But once you have stepped from darkness into light, it is now time to live out your faith. If there are no good deeds of fruit accompanying your faith in Christ, then the faith you have is dead!

What is the fruit that I am talking about? Read Galatians 5:22 and tell me if this is what you see coming out of your life. Are you producing:

- Love
- Joy
- Peace
- Patience
- Kindness
- Goodness
- Faithfulness
- Gentleness
- Self-Control

I run into Christian teenagers, at least they claim to be Christians, who are producing what you read about in Galatians 5:19-21. They are producing:

- Sexual Immorality
- Impurity
- Debauchery
- Idolatry
- Witchcraft
- Hatred
- Discord
- Jealousy

- Fits of rage
- Selfish Ambition
- Dissensions
- Factions
- Envy
- Drunkenness
- Orgies

What is coming out of your life? True faith shows itself in the life and actions that you are producing. I believe that Satan seeks to deceive us with a false faith. This is a belief that if you were confirmed or baptized that is good enough to get you into heaven. Go ahead and party all you want because you are saved. **I want to suggest that if you are living according to your old nature you ought to be questioning whether you are really saved.**

I want to lovingly give you a spiritual kick in the backside. It is time to wake up from your slumber and get on board. Have you trusted Christ with your eternity? Then you must start living for Him now by doing what He is asking you to do and stopping what He is asking you to stop. If you are not producing fruit and good deeds, then you have a faith that is dead and what good is that to anyone? It is no good to you because it isn't making a difference in your life and it is no good to others because you are not reaching out to care about them. Do you want to please God? Put Hebrews 13:16 into practice, *"And do not forget to do good and to share with others, for with such sacrifices God is pleased."*

## SOMETHING TO THINK ABOUT:

1. What is your life producing?

2. Is your faith alive and active or is it dead?

3. Do you even care?

## SOMETHING TO PRAY ABOUT:

Ask the Holy Spirit to begin to produce the fruit of the Spirit in your life. Tell Him that you will turn from the darkness and old nature. Ask Him to give you a brand new beginning.

## USE THIS SPACE TO JOURNAL ABOUT WHAT GOD IS SAYING TO YOU:

# DAY FORTY-TWO – JAMES 2:18

## SOMETHING TO STUDY:

*"But someone will say, 'You have faith; I have deeds'. Show me your faith without deeds, and I will show you my faith by what I do."*
James 2:18

Some say that they are "faith" Christians and some say that they are "deed" Christians. But James would say that is crazy because you can't separate the two; faith and deeds go hand in hand.

But if you could separate the two what would be better, to have faith without deeds or to show your faith by what you do? Obviously, it would be better to show your faith by the deeds you perform. What good does it do anyone if you have faith, but never live it out? Your faith was never meant to be a private thing that you hide on the inside. Your faith is something you give away, live out, and show to other people.

Someone might say, "You have faith in Jesus Christ, but you never live out your faith. I do not have faith in Christ, but I do a lot of good deeds and that will make me acceptable to God." Both stands are wrong. You are deceived if you think you can have faith in Jesus without good deeds. However, you are just as deceived if you try to gain God's acceptance because of good deeds. You will never gain salvation by your own works because you are a law breaker. Plus, listen to what God says about our good works in Isaiah 64:6, *"All of us have become like one who is unclean, and all our righteous acts are like filthy rags; we all shrivel up like a leaf, and like the wind our sins sweep us away."* **Even your best acts, apart from Jesus Christ, are like filthy rags.** You need Jesus to save you, forgive you, and lead you.

You can no longer live the way you want to live or act the way you want to act. This is no longer your life. You belong to Jesus Christ and He purchased your life. Please read 1 Corinthians 6:19-20 (notice that I said please) and see who is in charge of your life.

Notice that it says you are not your own, but you were bought with a price. So, what is the result of that? Do you live for yourself? No, you decide that you are going to honor God. One of the best ways to honor God is by a life well lived; you reach out to others in love and compassion.

What do non-Christians say is the number one reason they came to Christ? "I knew a Christian and their life so impressed me that I knew they had something that I didn't have and that led me to asking Christ into my life." What is the number one reason that non-Christians say they reject Christ? "I know other Christians and I don't see any difference between the way they live and the way I live." In other words, I know Christians, but I don't see them living out their faith. Are you setting a good or bad example?

## SOMETHING TO THINK ABOUT:

1. Who has been in charge of your life?

2. What would change if you surrendered completely to God?

3. Have you been deceived into thinking that your faith should be private, quiet,   and merely inward?

## SOMETHING TO PRAY ABOUT:

Ask God to make you bold in your faith. Ask Him for the courage to step out in faith and tell others about Him.

## USE THIS SPACE TO JOURNAL ABOUT WHAT GOD IS SAYING TO YOU:

# DAY FORTY-THREE – JAMES 2:19

## SOMETHING TO STUDY:

*"You believe that there is one God. Good! Even the demons believe that--and shudder."*
James 2:19

Do you realize that demons have faith? This is not a saving faith, but they do believe that there is a God, they believe that Jesus Christ was God in the flesh, they believe there is a heaven, and they believe many other things that atheists and agnostics would deny today.

I read this next part in a USA Today newspaper so you know it has to be true. In a poll, over 80% of teenagers claim to believe in God. That sounds really impressive until we read James 2:19 and realize that 100% of the demons believe in God and not one of them is going to heaven.

It is not enough to have an empty faith that says, "I believe in a God somewhere in the great cosmos." It is not good enough to merely have the faith of your mother or father. Your faith must be something that you own and are living out on a daily basis. I have both Catholic and Protestant friends who believe that being born into a Catholic/Protestant family and being confirmed or baptized is enough to get them into heaven even though Jesus Christ plays no part in their daily lives.

James is saying that it is good to believe in one God because that is the truth. But it needs to be more than just believing. **You need to reach out to Jesus Christ and decide if you are going to follow Him or not.**

If I decided to give you one thousand dollars cash, because I am a nice guy, and you say, "I really believe that Greg is going to give me that money." So I hold the money out and say, "Here it is." You say, "Yep, there it is." I say, "Here it is." You say, "There it is." Here, there, here, there. You will never have that money, no matter how much you believe, until you reach out and receive it.

Jesus Christ loves you. He died for you. He will be your best friend. He'll take good care of you now, and one day you can live with

Him forever in heaven. You say, "Wow, I really believe it." And Jesus says, "Great, here I am." You say, "Yep, there you are." And…I think you get the idea. You will never know Jesus Christ as your friend, Savior, and Lord until you reach out and receive Him into your life.

Have you made that choice and asked Christ into your life? This is the most important decision that you will ever make. You have a lot of decisions ahead of you. What college will you go to, what will you major in, and what kind of job will you get? Who will you marry and where will you live? But it is most important that you know where you are going to spend eternity. Can you know for sure that you are going to heaven? Yes, read 1 John 5:11-13. Do you know for sure that you are going to heaven?

## SOMETHING TO THINK ABOUT:

1. I want to spend eternity with YOU!

2. Have you talked to your friends about where they are going to spend eternity?

3. Jesus would rather go to hell for you than to heaven without you.

## SOMETHING TO PRAY ABOUT:

Ask Jesus to forgive you of your sins and to come into your life. Here is a simple prayer that, if this expresses the desire of your heart, you can pray now and Jesus will come into your life.
"Dear Jesus, I know I have made a lot of mistakes, some really poor choices and I have sinned. I need you and ask you to please forgive my sins and come into my life right now. Thank you for loving me, thank you that my sins are forgiven and thank you that you are in my life. I love you. In Jesus' name I pray. Amen!"
If you prayed that prayer please send me an e-mail and let me know: gregospeck@gmail.com

## USE THIS SPACE TO JOURNAL ABOUT WHAT GOD IS SAYING TO YOU:

# DAY FORTY-FOUR – JAMES 2:20-21

## SOMETHING TO STUDY:

*"You foolish man, do you want evidence that faith without deeds is useless? Was not our ancestor Abraham considered righteous for what he did when he offered his son Isaac on the altar?"*
James 2:20-21

If you think that you can have a true faith in Jesus Christ without good deeds, then you, my friend, are very, very foolish. Remember that faith and good deeds go together like peanut butter and jelly, macaroni and cheese, and the San Francisco 49ers and winning. Good deeds are a natural outpouring of your faith in Christ. **Belief in Jesus is a living faith, a practical faith, and a faith that moves a person to action.**

Some people get confused about this verse and think that Abraham was able to earn God's favor by offering his son, but you must look at the whole story of Abraham when reading this verse. Abraham first put his faith in God by moving himself, his servants, his animals, and his whole household to another country (Genesis 12:1-5). Then as an indication of his faith, he obediently offered his son as a sacrifice (Genesis 22:1-14) before the God in whom he already believed (Genesis 15:6). The righteous action of Abraham was evidence of his sincere and genuine faith.

We show faith every day in areas that have nothing to do with God. I fly somewhere almost every weekend. When I get on a plane I have faith in the pilot and the plane to get me where I need to go without crashing. If I thought the plane would crash, I wouldn't get on it. When I sit down in a chair I have faith that the chair will hold me. These are very minor areas compared with my faith in a God that will determine where I spend eternity.

Keep in mind that faith is only as good as the object it is trusting. You can have faith in your dog/cat to teach you algebra. That would be stupid because we all know that only dogs are smart enough to know algebra. You can build yourself some wings out of cardboard and have faith that when you jump off the mountain you will fly, but you won't, you will fall real fast. You won't do any real flying until you get to heaven!

Today a lot of people put their faith in things that are not worthy of their faith. False Gods and idols are leading people to hell. What good does it do to put your faith in a piece of stone to heal you? Or to ask some carved wood to save you?

Who can you trust completely to take care of you and want only what is best for you? Who can you trust completely with your eternity? There is only one person that is worthy of that kind of faith…Jesus Christ. Everyone will let you down and fall short of what you hoped they would be except for Jesus.

## SOMETHING TO THINK ABOUT:

1. Have you let go of your life and placed it in the hands of Jesus?

2. Are you living out your faith?

3. They will know we are Christians by our love.

## SOMETHING TO PRAY ABOUT:

Tell Jesus that you trust Him completely and will go wherever He wants you to go. Pray and place your life in His hands. Tell Him you will be a living sacrifice and that you want to be holy and pleasing in His sight.

## USE THIS SPACE TO JOURNAL ABOUT WHAT GOD IS SAYING TO YOU:

# DAY FORTY-FIVE – JAMES 2:22-23

## SOMETHING TO STUDY:

*"You see that his faith and his actions were working together, and his faith was made complete by what he did. And the scripture was fulfilled that says, 'Abraham believed God, and it was credited to him as righteousness,' and he was called God's friend."*
James 2:22-23

With Abraham, his faith and actions worked together. First he believed in God and then he backed up his beliefs with action. Remember that Abraham believed God back in Genesis 15:6, which was over thirty years before he offered Isaac to the Lord. So Abraham was accepted and saved by the Lord more than thirty years before this event James is talking about. When Abraham offered up Isaac, a result of his faith, he was adding works to his faith, just like we need to be doing each and every day.

Do you think that Abraham would have offered up Isaac if he hadn't already believed in God? No way, but because he had walked with God for the past thirty years, Abraham knew he could trust Him completely. Notice what Abraham said to Isaac in Genesis 22:8 when Isaac questioned him about where the offering is . . . *"God himself will provide the lamb for the burnt offering, my son."* He was willing to offer God his precious son because he knew God, trusted God, and had complete faith in Him.

Do you trust God completely and without reservation? How can you follow a God that you don't trust? The answer is that you can't and you will find yourself moving away from Jesus and toward the things of this world. You have to make the decision of whether you can trust Christ or not. **My experience tells me that you can trust Him totally, completely, and without reservation.** I am happy to place my life in His hands. No one loves and cares for us like He loves and cares for us. Will you ever experience pain if you trust Him? Yes. Will you ever suffer if you place your life in His hands? Yes. But you can be sure that He desires what is the very best for you and your life. The suffering you will face is temporary, but the glory, wonder, love, peace, joy, and happiness you will inherit is eternal.

Notice that Abraham was called God's friend. Wow, that is what I would like to be known as, Greg Speck--God's friend. Abraham was God's friend because he walked with Him, trusted Him, and lived for Him. That is something that you and I can do.

Guess what? Because of what Jesus Christ did for us on the cross, we are now a friend of God. That is the BEST! Since He is your friend, how should you treat a friend? How do you treat Jesus?

## SOMETHING TO THINK ABOUT:

1. If you struggle in your relationship with Christ, could it be because you don't really trust Him?

2. If you can't trust Him, then you won't follow Him.
3. Talk to someone about your doubts, concerns, and fears.

## SOMETHING TO PRAY ABOUT:

Tell God that you want to trust Him completely. Share with Him any fears and concerns that you have. Tell Him that you will choose to trust Him today.

## USE THIS SPACE TO JOURNAL ABOUT WHAT GOD IS SAYING TO YOU:

# DAY FORTY-SIX – JAMES 2:24

## SOMETHING TO STUDY:

*"You see that a person is justified by what he does and not by faith alone."*
James 2:24

What does the word justification mean? I will wait while you think…do you have an answer…are you ready? It means that God declares you right in His sight because of the price Jesus Christ paid for you on the cross. You have been released from the penalty of sin. Let's read Colossians 1:22 together, *"But now he has reconciled you by Christ's physical body through death to present you holy in his sight, without blemish and free from accusation--."* He is God the Father and the Father makes you right in His eyes because of Christ's death for you on the cross. He is now presenting you holy, without blemish, and free from accusation. When do you become holy, without blemish, and free from accusation? This happens the moment you ask Jesus Christ to become Savior and Lord of your life. This is not a process; it is an act of God. It is not something you do, it is something Christ does in you.

How can you tell if this has taken place? The person that comes to Christ has a changed life and there is a desire to trust and follow the Lord. Their faith is demonstrated by the good deeds that they do.

This goes back to James 2:17 where James is telling us that faith without works is dead. Do you think this is an important point? How many times has James said this same thing to us? He is saying that your life must prove your faith. You can't claim to love Jesus and then live for yourself. You can't say you are a child of the King and then live in sin.

What saves you is faith in God alone with no works added. But you show your friends, your parents, and your God that you are saved by works and without those works you have a dead faith.

Honestly, isn't that where many of us are, apathetic, pathetic and spiritually dead? Should that cause you any concern? Yes, it is time that you decide whether you are going to follow Jesus Christ or not. **Make a decision to either get in or get out, but get off the fence!**

127

Let's look at Revelation 3:15-16, *"I know your deeds, that you are neither cold nor hot. I wish you were either one or the other! So, because you are lukewarm-neither hot nor cold-I am about to spit you out of my mouth."* At the risk of sounding cold and uncaring, we would be better off if some who profess to be Christians just left the faith. We have too many within the Body of Christ who are compromising and setting terrible examples. So my comment to them is to get out. You decide, be hot or be cold, but stop being lukewarm. By riding the fence, you are causing more damage than doing good for the cause of Christ.

## SOMETHING TO THINK ABOUT:

1. Are your actions backing up your faith?

2. Are you hot or cold or are you lukewarm?

3. What does it mean that God is going to spit the lukewarm out of His mouth?

## SOMETHING TO PRAY ABOUT:

Ask God to continue to give you sensitivity to the needs around you. Ask Him to give you the resources to meet those needs. Tell Him that you want to be hot and not lukewarm.

## USE THIS SPACE TO JOURNAL ABOUT WHAT GOD IS SAYING TO YOU:

# DAY FORTY-SEVEN – JAMES 2:25

## SOMETHING TO STUDY

*"In the same way, was not even Rahab the prostitute considered righteous for what she did when she gave lodging to the spies and sent them off in a different direction?"*
James 2:25

First, Rahab believed in God and then she acted upon her faith with good works. You can read the whole story in Joshua 2:1-21 and 6:22-23, but let me point out a few verses.

In verse 9, Rahab sends the guards away who were looking for the spies and then goes back to the spies and says *"I know that the Lord has given this land to you and that a great fear of you has fallen on us, so that all who live in this country are melting in fear because of you."* She continues in verse 11, *"When we heard of it, our hearts melted and everyone's courage failed because of you, for the Lord your God is God in heaven above and on the earth below."* Here is a declaration of faith by Rahab. This is especially amazing because she had grown up with other gods her whole life, plus Jericho had never fallen to an enemy. However, Rahab now believes that the God of the Israelites is the God of heaven and earth. To prove her faith, she hid the spies and helped them escape. Her faith was an active and practical faith. It was a faith that saved not only her, but also her entire family.

Why list a prostitute with Abraham? Doesn't that sound a little strange to you? I think it is very cool because James is giving us two extremes. First there is Abraham the father of nations and then you have Rahab the prostitute. Why is that so cool is because we all fall between those two people. **No one is excluded by God and there is hope for all of us.**

Did you know that Rahab is in the genealogy of Jesus? Read Matthew 1:5 and realize that Jesus descended from a prostitute. Have you fallen beyond the arms of Jesus? Are you beyond saving, changing, and restoring? No! If God can change a prostitute and use her in the line of King David and Jesus Christ, then He can certainly save you and change your life. God has a purpose and a destiny for your life. Why would you want anything less than His very best?

129

You have done some things that you are ashamed of, I have done some things that I am ashamed of, and Rahab did some things that she was ashamed of. Jesus is ready, willing, and able to forgive, restore, and use us. Run to the Lord and you will discover an amazing thing will happen. God the Father will run to you. That is how much He really, really loves you!

## SOMETHING TO THINK ABOUT:

1. Why would you ever want to wander away from Jesus?

2. If God can change a prostitute, do you think He can change you?

3. God has forgiven us ALL our sins!

## SOMETHING TO PRAY ABOUT:

Thank God that He chose to save you and adopt you into His family. Ask Him to lead you into your destiny and the plans that He has for you. Tell Him that you will accept His will for your life.

## USE THIS SPACE TO JOURNAL ABOUT WHAT GOD IS SAYING TO YOU:

# DAY FORTY-EIGHT – JAMES 2:26

## SOMETHING TO STUDY:

*"As the body without the spirit is dead, so faith without deeds is dead."*
James 2:26

Do you get what God is trying to say to you through James? Do you finally understand…hello…do you get it…is anyone home? Let me say it again, if you believe in Jesus Christ and claim to have faith, then you must be living out that faith day to day. You must be doing good works because faith without works is dead!

Faith is very important to God because… *"Faith is being sure of what we hope for and certain of what we do not see,"* (Hebrews 11:1). *"By faith we understand that the universe was formed at God's command…"* (Hebrews 11:3a*)*. *"…Without faith it is impossible to please God, because anyone who comes to him must believe that he exists and that he rewards those who earnestly seek him,"* (Hebrews 11:6).

Which is the best Hall of Fame to be a part of: football, baseball, basketball, hockey, NASCAR, bowling, wrestling, or left handed ping pong players who grew up in North Dakota? None of the above! The best Hall of Fame to be a part of is the Faith Hall Fame. You will discover the list of inductees in Hebrews 11 and you will also notice that the actions of each person followed their faith in God. Here are a few examples: By faith…

- Abel offered a sacrifice to God.
- Noah built an ark.
- Abraham made his home in the Promised Land.
- Isaac blessed Jacob and Esau.
- Moses led the children of Israel out of Egypt.
- Gideon, Barak, Samson, Jephthah, David, Samuel, and what about you?

Your future could hold your induction into the Hall of Faith. Here are some modern day men and women that will be entering the Hall: Billy Graham, Bill Bright, Jim Elliott, Elizabeth Elliott, D.L. Moody, and countless missionaries that have faithfully served the Lord.

Many are unknown to us, but they are not unknown to heaven and one day we will know about them.

**You can be a hero of the faith.** One day your name can be entered into the Hall of Faith. What will it take for that to happen? You need to be faithful and available. Going where God wants you to go, doing what God wants you to do, and being controlled by the Holy Spirit. I believe that you can do that and you can begin that journey today.

## SOMETHING TO THINK ABOUT:

1. Have you ever considered that you could be a member of the Hall of Faith?

2. Who have you heard of or known that has tremendous faith?

3. What is stopping you from stepping out in faith and living for Jesus?

## SOMETHING TO PRAY ABOUT:

Ask God for faith to be able to trust Him completely. Pray for God to move in powerful ways. Ask Him to use you to make a difference in your world.

## USE THIS SPACE TO JOURNAL ABOUT WHAT GOD IS SAYING TO YOU:

# DAY FORTY-NINE – JAMES 3:1

## SOMETHING TO STUDY:

*"Not many of you should presume to be teachers, my brothers, because you know that we who teach will be judged more strictly."*
James 3:1

They say that great minds deal with philosophies, ideas, and the truths of God's Word. Average minds look at what is happening around them and discuss the events of the day: "Hey how about those (fill in with your favorite sports team)." While small minds center on and gossip about people. What kind of minds do you see filling your youth group and church? What kind of mind do you have? I think that most churches are made up of small minds that would rather tear people down than seek to understand God's Word. This whole journey through James is meant to build our minds and help us practically live out God's Word in our lives.

James is talking to us about being careful if you are a teacher because you will be judged more strictly. A teacher is telling people how they should live, what God is calling them to do, and if they haven't lived up to God's standard. A teacher is seeking to mentor those who are listening and sitting under the teaching. So, God is holding the teacher responsible to live out what they are telling other people to do. Teaching is a high calling and should not be taken lightly. Read 1 Corinthians 12:28 and notice that teaching ranks number three behind apostles and prophets. It is something very important to God and it should be important to us.

Teaching is not something that you do if you can't think of anything else to do. Being a teacher is something that God calls you into and you seek to be obedient to that call in your life. It is a great honor to be called into teaching, but it is also an awesome responsibility and should not be taken lightly. If you are going to teach, then keep these things in mind:

- You must be surrendered to the control of the Holy Spirit. You can teach on your own power and be informative, motivating, and humorous, but it won't be life changing. Only God can change a life and that will only occur if the Lord is working in and through you.

- You must have a consistent devotional life. You need to be men and women that study the Word, not for message preparation, but for personal application.
- You must be teachable and open to correction and guidance.
- You must have studied the Word of God and prepared yourself to communicate God's truth to those who are listening. Check out 1 Timothy 1:7, *"They want to be teachers of the law, but they do not know what they are talking about or what they so confidently affirm."*
- Realize that the most important part of your teaching is God's Word and not the stories, illustrations, jokes, and applications that you will seek to bring to the message. Do I use humor, illustrations, and application? Yes, but I remember that it is most important to have people seeing the truth of the Word of God.
- You must be living out what you are teaching. You can't say, "Do what I say and not what I do."
- Realize that God is going to hold you to a higher standard. If you don't want to be judged more strictly, then don't become a teacher.

Do not fear the responsibility of teaching God's truth. If He has called you to be a teacher, then He will give you the gifts, talents, and power to do what He is calling you to do. If you refuse to teach, you are going outside of His will for your life. Be faithful to His calling and He will take care of you. **You will never be happier than when you are doing exactly what God has called you to do.** I love teaching and preaching and I can't imagine doing anything else. But at the same time, I realize that I better behave myself. We are all called to live a life that will bring honor and glory to our Lord Jesus Christ. This is especially true for teachers.

Do you have to be perfect to teach? No, I make mistakes all the time and fall into sin. However, I deal with the sin immediately and I don't allow it to fester and destroy me on the inside. It is really a matter of your heart. Do you desire to follow and serve the Lord or are you pursuing the things of the world? Again, you go into teaching because this is what God is telling you to do and not because it is meeting needs in your life for attention. There are some people that go into youth ministry because they need to be needed and they think this will help them feel better about themselves. That is the wrong reason to work with teenagers and the wrong reason to want to be a teacher.

What should you do if your Youth Pastor asks you to teach at youth group? Ask yourself the question, "Am I loving Jesus Christ and staying away from willful sin?" If the answer is yes, then go ahead and teach. If we had to wait until we were perfect before we taught, then none of us would be teaching. But if you are living a lie and your heart is far from the Lord, do not teach! You can fool your Youth Pastor, but you can't fool God and you aren't fooling some of the students that see right through your masks.

For you who are called to be teachers, I would tell you to read 2 Timothy 4:1-5.

*"In the presence of God and of Christ Jesus, who will judge the living and the dead, and in view of his appearing and his kingdom, I give you this charge: Preach the Word; be prepared in season and out of season; correct, rebuke and encourage--with great patience and careful instruction. For the time will come when men will not put up with sound doctrine. Instead, to suit their own desires, they will gather around them a great number of teachers to say what their itching hears want to hear. They will turn their ears away from the truth and turn aside to myths. But you, keep your head in all situations, endure hardship, do the work of an evangelist, discharge all the duties of your ministry."*

If God calls you to be a teacher, be a teacher with integrity and the courage to preach the Word of God even if people don't want to hear it.

**SOMETHING TO THINK ABOUT:**

1. What comes out of your mouth reveals what you are really like on the inside.

2. Is God calling you to teach?

3. How close are you to Jesus right now?

**SOMETHING TO PRAY ABOUT:**

Ask God what He wants you to do. Ask Him if He wants you to teach. Tell Him that you are willing to do anything that He asks you to do. Once again surrender your life to the control of the Holy Spirit.

**USE THIS SPACE TO JOURNAL ABOUT WHAT GOD IS SAYING TO YOU:**

# DAY FIFTY – JAMES 3:2

## SOMETHING TO STUDY:

*"We all stumble in many ways. If anyone is never at fault in what he says, he is a perfect man, able to keep his whole body in check."*
James 3:2

Do you find yourself falling into the same sin over and over again? In what areas do you slip up and fall? James tells us, "We all stumble in many ways." That says we all continue to mess up and make bad choices. It also says that there is more than one area we struggle with. The first step in experiencing victory over sin is identifying your areas of weakness.

Secondly, you need to watch what comes out of your mouth. Does that sound weird to you? James says that if you are never at fault in what you say then you are a perfect person and able to keep your whole body under control. How can that be? Check out Matthew 12:34-37 and tell me what that is saying to you. It says to me that my mouth reveals my heart and what is going on inside of me. If my words are kind and loving, that is an indication that my insides are pure and pleasing to the Lord. If I am never at fault in what I say, I am looking really good on the inside and I have become the perfect man.

However, my mouth is not always pleasing to the Lord and it gets me in trouble sometimes. Even heroes of the faith struggle with the words that come out of their mouths. Abraham lied. Peter denied Jesus Christ three times. Elijah complained and asked to die. Jonah was upset that God had shown mercy to a city and didn't destroy it (of course he was real happy that God had shown him mercy just before this). All through history, men and women have struggled with their tongues.

Remember when we talked about the fruit of the Spirit? We determined this is a good way to check the words that are coming out of your mouth. Are your words loving, full of joy, peaceful, patient, kind, good, faithful to the Lord, gentle, and under control?

Can this ever happen? Yes, if you're controlled and empowered by the Holy Spirit. He will lead you to do, read, see, and act in ways that are pleasing to the Lord. What you are taking into your life will impact your words. What you put into your mind goes into your heart and then comes out of your mouth.

Your spiritual maturity can be measured by what comes out of your mouth. You can tell me that you have known Jesus for many years, memorized boat loads of verses, and have gone on numerous missions trips, but if your words are sick, your life is sick. Do you want to clean up your life? Start with your words. **Keep your mouth under control and your life will follow.**

## SOMETHING TO THINK ABOUT:

1. Could the areas that you are stumbling in be the direct result of what you are taking into your life?

2. What have your words been like over the past week?

3. Your tongue speaks what your life has experienced.

## SOMETHING TO PRAY ABOUT:

Ask God to make you sensitive to what you are taking into your life. Tell Him that you want to honor Him by what comes out of your mouth today.

## USE THIS SPACE TO JOURNAL ABOUT WHAT GOD IS SAYING TO YOU:

# DAY FIFTY-ONE – JAMES 3:3-5a

## SOMETHING TO STUDY:

*"When we put bits into the mouths of horses to make them obey us, we can turn the whole animal. Or take ships as an example. Although they are so large and are driven by strong winds, they are steered by a very small rudder wherever the pilot wants to go. Likewise the tongue is a small part of the body, but it makes great boasts."*
James 3:3-5a

I have only ridden a horse a few times in my life. I was speaking at a summer camp and the head wrangler said, "I will take you out for a ride, just the two of us." That sounded okay to me so we met that afternoon. The wrangler gave me some instructions including don't hold onto the horn. Everything was going great until he asked me if I wanted to cantor. I thought cantor meant to trot so I said, "sure!" He told me to gently kick the side of the horse, but when I did that the horse took off like it was shot out of a cannon! The first thing I did was grab onto the horn and hang on for dear life! As my life flashed before my eyes, I noticed that the horse had a small bit in its mouth. I could make the horse turn right or left or stop with the reins that were attached to that little bit. Well, maybe I couldn't quite stop it. After our cantor through the woods, my backside hurt for two days!

Now, notice how small the rudder is compared to the ship as a whole. It is very small, but with a rudder you can make a ship, a huge ship, turn left or right or make it go straight ahead. If the rudder is broken the ship is in big trouble.

What about your tongue? How big is it compared to the rest of your body? It is very small and seemingly insignificant. But with that tongue, we end up making great boasts that can turn our lives away from the straight and narrow path. Psalm 94:4 says, "They pour out arrogant words; all the evildoers are full of boasting."

What do we boast about? There are too many to mention them all, but let me list a few:

- They boast of the **cravings of their heart** according to Psalm 10:3. What would that include? How about sex, drugs, shop-lifting, drinking, partying, speeding, lying, cheating, or rebelling? I am sure you could add to this list. Keep in mind, not only does this person desire these things, but they also boast about it. They are bragging about doing evil or at least craving it. I see these students that do this all the time. The media portrays people that celebrate what is evil and boast about their sin as adventurous and fun.

- They boast of their **wealth** in Psalm 49:6. Money has become their God and all their time is spent making money or thinking about making money. Wealth has become their idol and they want everyone to know that they are wealthy. I am sure that you know people who seek wealth more than they seek anything else.

- They boast of **all they have or can do** but it is described as empty boasting in Proverbs 25:14. Here the person boasts about stuff that they don't deliver on. I have this or I can do that, but you never see it happen. A lot of talk and promises, but no follow through. During my freshman year at Bethel University, there was a guy living on my floor who had football trophies all over his room. He looked like a very impressive person. He told us that he didn't go out for the football team because he wanted to concentrate on his studies. After boasting about what a great player he was, he couldn't even make the starting lineup for our intramural football team. It turned out that this guy had the trophies he made for himself to try to impress those around him. He was boasting about something he had never done and he could never deliver on any of his promises.

- They boast about **tomorrow and everything that they are going to do** according to Proverbs 27:1. The truth is that you have no idea what is going to happen tomorrow. You aren't even guaranteed that you will be around tomorrow. It's not important what you want to do with your life, but what God wants to do with your life. **Live for Jesus today and trust Him for your tomorrows.** Allow God to direct your steps. If you boast about what you are going to do and then don't end up doing it, you can look pretty foolish.

What should you boast about? Here is what the Bible says:

- Psalm 34:2, *"My soul will boast in the Lord..."*

- Psalm 44:8, *"In God we make our boast all day long, and we will praise your name forever."*

- 2 Corinthians 10:17-18, *"But, let him who boasts, boast in the Lord. For it is not the one who commends himself who is approved, but the one whom the Lord commends."*

- 2 Corinthians 11:30, *"If I must boast, I will boast of the things that show my weakness."*

- 2 Corinthians 12:9-10, *"My grace is sufficient for you, for my power is made perfect in weakness.' Therefore I will boast all the more gladly about my weaknesses, so that Christ's power may rest on me. That is why, for Christ's sake, I delight in weaknesses, in insults, in hardships, in persecutions, in difficulties. For when I am weak, then I am strong."*

If you are going to boast, boast about what God has been doing in your life-- all the things that He has been teaching you and all He has revealed to you. Boast of your weaknesses and the need you have for Jesus to be in control of your life. In your weakness, you are strong if you surrender to God. Give God the glory before man, let others know that you love and depend on Him.

We place a bit in the mouth of a horse so that we can control the animal. An out of control horse can be a scary thing and is capable of great damage to you and others. We use a small rudder to control a big ship. Without the rudder, the ship sails out of control and can do a lot of damage to the passengers, crew, and anything in its way. We too must have our tongue under control or we can do a lot of damage to God's name, our reputation, and to others.

The tongue reflects our lives and makes great boasts for good or evil. With our tongue we make God look very good or with our tongue we make God look very bad. With our tongue we draw people closer to the person of Jesus Christ or with our tongue we drive people away. With our tongue we make friends or create enemies. Our tongue

141

is very small, but it makes a huge impact. What has your tongue been doing this past week?

## SOMETHING TO THINK ABOUT:

1. Why is the tongue like a mirror?

2. What have you been boasting about?

3. Why is it good to be weak?

## SOMETHING TO PRAY ABOUT:

Ask God to give you opportunities to boast about Him and what He has done in your life. Surrender your tongue to Him and ask Him to control it.

## USE THIS SPACE TO JOURNAL ABOUT WHAT GOD IS SAYING TO YOU:

# DAY FIFTY-TWO – JAMES 3:5b-6

## SOMETHING TO STUDY:

*"Consider what a great forest is set on fire by a small spark. The tongue also is a fire, a world of evil among the parts of the body. It corrupts the whole person, sets the whole course of his life on fire, and is itself set on fire by hell."*
James 3:5b-6

I love the fact that God doesn't beat around the bush. He simply tells you exactly what you need to hear. The tongue is a very small part of your body, but it has the potential of doing tremendous damage to you and those around you. Consider the following:

- Every summer we hear reports of forest fires that destroy thousands of acres. What caused it? Too often it is because of a careless person who dropped a match or cigarette. One small spark can destroy thousands of miles.
- I live near Chicago and have heard the story of Mrs. O'Leary's cow. According to tradition, the cow kicked over a lamp in the barn on October 8, 1871 at 8:30p.m. The fire spread through Chicago and over 100,000 people were left homeless, over 300 were killed and more than 17,000 buildings were destroyed. All this destruction because one cow kicked over one lamp in a barn.

Even though the tongue is small it can also cause damage to hundreds of people, thousands of miles away. Just think of the damage that you have done with your tongue.

Have you ever…
- Hurt your parents by something you said?
- Made a sibling mad?
- Damaged a friendship?
- Insulted a waitress, cashier, teller, etc.?
- Scarred someone's reputation?
- Started a fight with someone?
- Caused someone to cry?
- Said something that you later regretted?

I have done all that and more, except make a sibling mad. I am proud to say that I have never made one of my brothers or sister mad, because I am an only child. The tongue, out of control, will cause damage that can last a lifetime. Words have caused wars, destroyed friendships, busted up marriages, led to fist fights and even resulted in murder.

Fire can be terrific or it can be terrifying. Last night I started a fire in our fireplace, put on some music, poured myself a hot drink and read a good book. The fire was tremendous. It was warm, inviting and comforting. But take that same fire and put it in the middle of the bedroom and all of the sudden it becomes horrible, painful and destructive.

In the same way, **words can be terrific or terrifying.** With my words I can build up, comfort and encourage those around me. But with the same mouth I can use words to attack, tear down and destroy someone else. Your words lead you toward peace or anger, life or death, purity or immorality, love or lust, good or evil, joy or depression, character or corruption, trust or jealousy, generosity or greed. Which direction are your words leading you?

Notice that today's verse says the tongue corrupts the whole person. How is this possible? Keep in mind that you can't hurt someone else without hurting yourself. By being mean to someone else, you are hurting yourself emotionally and spiritually. Hurtful and hateful words cause you to be cold, hard and uncaring on the inside. It does not please God and you feel your relationship with Him drifting apart.

In addition, a fire builds and becomes more intense consuming everything in its path without thought to the consequences. In the same way, your words can escalate and become angrier and crueler. You become louder and soon you are out of control like a raging forest fire. This can lead you to say things that you deeply regret and the hurt you are causing others hurts you too.

Remember, a fire needs fuel to keep going. Without the wood or other materials the forest fire goes out. Check out these verses that speak about the fire of the tongue.

Proverbs 26:20: *"Without wood a fire goes out; without gossip a quarrel dies down."*

Proverbs 26:21: *"As charcoal to embers and as wood to fire, so is a quarrelsome man for kindling strife."*

Ephesians 4:31: *"Get rid of all bitterness, rage and anger, brawling and slander, along with every form of malice."*

1 Peter 2:1: *"Therefore, rid yourselves of all malice and all deceit, hypocrisy, envy and slander of every kind."*

Now, take your Bible and read Proverbs 10. Underline anything that has to do with the tongue. Write down what God is saying to you through these verses. There is a lot of good stuff!

Who wants to see your tongue set on fire so it can do all the damage that it has the potential to do? Satan. He is the one who wants to see your tongue out of control. Hell sets the tongue on fire! The enemy is aware that with your words you can disgrace Jesus Christ, push people away from the good news and destroy relationships and individuals. What better way to destroy you and others than by your very words? He tempts you to say what is wrong and then accuses you and shames you for saying what he wanted you to say. He is the master deceiver and manipulator. He can emotionally, spiritually and sometimes physically destroy you and others by merely using your words.

However, you have a choice of who is going to be in control of your tongue. You are not caught between two equal superpowers. Greater is Jesus Christ, who is in you, than Satan who is in the world. There is no power struggle going on between God and Satan. God is omnipotent and in control. Satan has no power or control over God. So surrender yourself, and specifically your tongue, to the Lord and let Him know that it is your desire to honor Him with everything that comes out of it. He will give you the power to talk the way you ought to talk. The Holy Spirit will fill you and control you so that your words bring life and not death.

## SOMETHING TO THINK ABOUT:

1. How have your words impacted people this week?

2. If you hurt others you are hurting yourself. Do you see that?

3. Your words will either draw people closer to Jesus or push them farther away.

## SOMETHING TO PRAY ABOUT:

Ask God to use you and your words to bring joy, peace and healing to the people around you. Ask Him to use you to build people up and not tear them down. Ask Him to keep you away from gossip.

## USE THIS SPACE TO JOURNAL ABOUT WHAT GOD IS SAYING TO YOU:

# DAY FIFTY-THREE – JAMES 3:7-8

## SOMETHING TO STUDY:

*"All kinds of animals, birds, reptiles and creatures of the sea are being tamed and have been tamed by man, but no man can tame the tongue. It is a restless evil, full of deadly poison."*
James 3:7-8

We had the best dog in the world. My friend Brian Erickson trained Taylor and this dog was amazing. I could go on a walk with her and she would stay right next to me without a leash. She never jumped up on people or the furniture and she was a total lover. Taylor was part golden retriever and part black lab. You could give her a command and she would do it immediately. Sit down, roll over, fetch the paper, fix my breakfast, Taylor could do it all! People have trained all kinds of animals, birds, reptiles and creatures of the sea, but we have never been able to train the tongue.

The tongue is a restless evil always looking for an opportunity to attack and destroy. It can spin out of control and begin to control us. One of the problems is that the tongue takes on so many disguises. At times it even fools us! What are some of the disguises the tongue takes on?

- Sometimes I exaggerate-This is called lying. You seek to make things worse, better, bigger or smaller. You want to tell an exciting story so everyone will be amazed. I have been with teens that have told me these wild tales of things they have done or things done to them. Some of it was the truth but some was an exaggeration and that is lying.

- I get a little lazy with all the facts-You are telling the truth to a point, but you are not telling everything. In other words, you are deceiving a person and that is lying. When you gossip or listen to someone gossip, do you tell or hear the whole story? No, you are only telling or hearing one side of the story. Gossips are trying to make themselves look good and the other person look bad.

- I don't say anything wrong, I just like to talk-You talk non-stop and you never shut your mouth. When I am with these kinds of people I want to say to them, "Take a breath!" Someone asks what time it is and this person tells them all about the watch they are wearing. When you talk too much you drive people away from you. I have had some friends that talk too much and I have tried to lovingly point that out to them and either they don't see it or don't care, because they just keep on talking. What did James teach us earlier in 1:19? Be slow to speak so that you can be quick to listen.

- I help people by pointing out their weaknesses-As iron sharpens iron, so we sharpen each other. This is good, but it is easy to take it a step too far and become negative and critical. There is no place for being rude or cruel as Christians. Think about how you feel when others point out your weaknesses. I believe it is more effective to catch people being good and point out their strengths instead of focusing on their weaknesses.

- I share negative stuff that other people are doing so that we can pray for them-Prayer is important and powerful, but it is not to be used as an excuse to gossip. It is wrong for you to share the sins and mistakes of others under the guise of needing to pray for them. You can pray for individuals without getting into details about what they are doing.

- I like to flatter people-It is good to build others up and encourage them, but insincere praise is bad because you are giving people an unrealistic picture of themselves.

- I use strong language to get my point across-There is no excuse for using profanity or being rude and insensitive. If you can't get your point across without compromising in this area, then the problem lies with you and not others. You can say something with intensity, but your words need to first and foremost honor God.

- I just say what I am thinking, at least I am being honest-You must think before you speak or you will end up saying a lot of things that are hurting other people or making you look stupid or probably both. Honesty must always be mixed with love or it is sin. Honesty without love is being rude and insulting and love without honesty is deception.

148

Do you recognize yourself in any of these disguises that the tongue can take on? To deal with it you first need to see it and then you can make the changes God is calling you to make. Remember, you are always just one step away from saying something that you will deeply regret and can leave others with deep emotional scars.

The tongue is full of deadly poison. You don't see poison work like you would see a gunshot or knife wound. It attacks the inside, sometimes quickly, sometimes slowly, killing the other person. So the tongue hits hardest on the inside where no one else sees and slowly or quickly kills the person emotionally and spiritually. I can remember things that were said to me when I was little that hurt me emotionally. I bet you can remember some hurtful things that were said to you. That should remind us how powerful words are and how they can continue to hurt years and decades later. I remember what my Mom would say when a person said something mean to me, "Sticks and stone may break my bones, but words will never hurt me." This is stupid and wrong. I would much rather be hit by a rock than a cruel word.

Do you know who can be some of the cruelest people? Other Christians can be some of the rudest and meanest people around. I have never had non-Christians come close to saying things as hurtful as what Christians have said. Part of the problem might be that I expect non-Christians to be mean, but not my brothers and sisters in Christ.

Now here is the exciting news! **No man can tame the tongue, but God can tame the tongue.** I want you to do three things.

- Surrender your tongue to the control of the Holy Spirit.
- Ask God to guard your lips (Psalm 14:3).
- Seek to actively please God with your words (Psalm 19:14).

## SOMETHING TO THINK ABOUT:

1. When it comes to the tongue, where do you see yourself stumbling?

2. Who is in control of your tongue?

3. Is your tongue full of life or poison?

**SOMETHING TO PRAY ABOUT:**

Ask God to show you any bad disguises your tongue has been taking on and tell Him you want to honor Him and build others up with your words.

**USE THIS SPACE TO JOURNAL ABOUT WHAT GOD IS SAYING TO YOU:**

# DAY FIFTY-FOUR – JAMES 3:9

## SOMETHING TO STUDY:

*"With the tongue we praise our Lord and Father, and with it we curse
men, who have been made in God's likeness."*
James 3:9

We show up on Sunday or Saturday and sing praises to the
Lord and lift up prayers of worship and adoration. But then on Monday
someone cuts us off as we are driving to school and we unload words
that grieve the Lord. We get in the locker room and tell stories that our
parents would be shocked at. Does this seem hypocritical to you? It
does to me and I do this very thing. I praise my Father in heaven and
then bad mouth others that are creations of my heavenly Father.

Do you love God, I mean really love God? Are you having
trouble being kind and loving to people around you? Please read these
verses carefully and make sure that you mark them in your Bible. 1
John 4:20-21 says, *"If anyone says, 'I love God,' yet hates his brother,
he is a liar. For anyone who does not love his brother, whom he has
seen, cannot love God, whom he has not seen. And he has given us this
command: Whoever loves God must also love his brother."* What do
these two verses say to you? It says to me that if I am going to love
God, I better also be loving people around me.

Have I mentioned that I am at my worst behind the wheel of a
car? That is an area that I desperately need to work on in my own life. I
can be coming out of a wonderful time of ministry where God worked
in awesome ways and get mad at someone in another car. We are all in
the process of growing, learning and changing. Here is an area that I
need to work on and continue to surrender to the Lord. If you are going
to change then you must first be able to see your weaknesses and then
have a willing heart to change those areas that do not please God.

What if you decided to spend the day being nice to people and
doing random acts of kindness? We have enjoyed doing this as a family.
Here is some of the stuff we have done in the past...

- To drive in Illinois you have to pay tolls, so pay for the
  car behind you.

- Pick a couple or family in a restaurant and pay for their meal.
- Smile and say hi to as many people as you can. I would suggest that girls greet girls and guys greet guys so we don't give off the wrong signal.
- Give someone an anonymous encouraging note.
- Compliment someone who has been serving you like a waiter or waitress.
- Ask for the manager to tell them something nice about an employee.
- Pick up some litter.
- As you fix your coffee in the café, clean off the counter for the next person.
- Now be creative and add to this list.

## SOMETHING TO THINK ABOUT:

1. How have you been treating the people around you?

2. If you love God, you must also love others.

3. **We lie with our lips and we lie with our life.**

## SOMETHING TO PRAY ABOUT:

Ask God to give you a love and compassion for those around you. Tell Him that you love Him and want to serve Him by loving those people that He has created.

## USE THIS SPACE TO JOURNAL ABOUT WHAT GOD IS SAYING TO YOU:

# DAY FIFTY-FIVE – JAMES 3:10-12

## SOMETHING TO STUDY:

*"Out of the same mouth come praise and cursing. My brothers, this should not be. Can both fresh water and salt water flow from the same spring? My brothers, can a fig tree bear olives, or a grapevine bear figs? Neither can a salt spring produce fresh water."*
James 3:10-12

Do you find a spring that produces fresh and salt water? Do you see a fig tree that is producing olives or a grapevine that has figs on it? NO! So our mouths should not be producing curses. God has made our mouth to praise Him and to build up others.

We have talked about steps that you can take and things that you can do, but if your tongue is inconsistent then there is something wrong with your heart! **Out of the heart your mouth speaks, so work on your heart and you will be helping your mouth.** How do you work on your heart? Be careful about what you are taking into your life; the things that you listen to, watch, and read are all having an impact on you for good or for evil. Here are some verses that continue to speak to us about the tongue:

Psalm 34:13-14: *"Keep your tongue from evil and your lips from speaking lies. Turn from evil and do good; seek peace and pursue it."*

Proverbs 13:3: *"He who guards his lips guards his life, but he who speaks rashly will come to ruin."*

Proverbs 21:23: *"He who guards his mouth and his tongue keeps himself from calamity."*

1 Peter 3:8-10: *"Finally, all of you, live in harmony with one another; be sympathetic, love as brothers, be compassionate and humble. Do not repay evil with evil or insult with insult, but with blessing, because to this you were called so that you may inherit a blessing. For, 'Whoever would love life and see good days must keep his tongue from evil and his lips from deceitful speech'."*

Notice here that you have a choice when people insult you. You can respond to an insult with an insult or you can give a blessing. I want to suggest that you and I need to respond to evil with good and give a blessing instead of an insult. When we do that, I think at least three things happen:

- We smash their expectations. They don't expect that blessing.
- We open them to self-examination. Because we didn't respond to them the way they expected, it gets them to start thinking about their words and actions.
- It releases the Holy Spirit to work in their lives.

Romans 12:21 says *"Do not be overcome by evil, but overcome evil with good."* Try doing that today.

## SOMETHING TO THINK ABOUT:

1. Have you ever responded to an insult with a blessing?

2. Blessings must be given without sarcasm.

3. Blessing holds the hope of changed lives.

## SOMETHING TO PRAY ABOUT:

Ask God to remind you to give a blessing the next time you are insulted. Ask Him to purify your heart so that your mouth can bring forth praises and words of affirmation.

## USE THIS SPACE TO JOURNAL ABOUT WHAT GOD IS SAYING TO YOU:

# DAY FIFTY-SIX – JAMES 3:13

## SOMETHING TO STUDY:

*"Who is wise and understanding among you? Let him show it by his good life, by deeds done in the humility that comes from wisdom."*
James 3:13

Do you desire to be wise and understanding? First of all, remember that wisdom comes from God. If you want wisdom, then you need to ask Him and He will freely give it to you. But how can you tell if you have received that wisdom? This verse gives us two ways of telling, and it's really pretty easy.

First of all, we need to be living the good life. Now I am not talking about cruising on your own personal yacht, having a villa in the Alps and a bank account the size of our national debt. That is not the good life that James is talking about. He is talking about a life well lived, a life that honors and glorifies Jesus Christ. That life may not include a yacht, villa or big bank account, but it will give you a great retirement plan where you store up treasures in heaven that can never be taken away from you!

Being wise and understanding is not primarily about knowing facts and information, but about living correctly. Abby is a friend of mine who is a junior in high school. She is sick and tired of meeting everyone's expectations of her as a Christian. So she is ready to kiss Christianity goodbye. I told her, "Don't allow others to manipulate you and keep you away from Jesus. Don't be concerned about being what others expect you to be, just be what God is calling you to be and live a life that is pleasing to Him."

Do you have wisdom and understanding? If so, you are living a life that is pleasing to the Lord. Talk is cheap and you must back up your words with action. **To love Jesus is to live for Jesus.**

The second indicator of wisdom and understanding is humility. Humility is not weakness, but it is strength under control. It means you are kind, caring, gentle, considerate, wise and understanding. A humble person cares about people no matter how they look, dress or smell. A humble person stands against evil and what is wrong. Remember that evil wins when good does nothing. Humility is strong and courageous and does not bow to evil. You see the needs around you and you do something about it.

Today we look for a cause to fight for and something to champion. There is no greater cause than the cause of Christ. Ephesians 4:1-3 will sum everything up for us, *"As a prisoner for the Lord, then, I urge you to live a life worthy of the calling you have received. Be completely humble and gentle; be patient, bearing with one another in love. Make every effort to keep the unity of the Spirit through the bond of peace."* If you do this, you will show everyone that you are a man or woman of wisdom and understanding!

## SOMETHING TO THINK ABOUT:

1. Do you have wisdom and understanding?

2. You can get all A's on your report card and not have wisdom or understanding.

3. How have you shown humility this week?

## SOMETHING TO PRAY ABOUT:

Tell God that you want to be someone who is wise and understanding. Tell Him you want to live a life pleasing to Him.

## USE THIS SPACE TO JOURNAL ABOUT WHAT GOD IS SAYING TO YOU:

# DAY FIFTY-SEVEN – JAMES 3:14

## SOMETHING TO STUDY:

*"But if you harbor bitter envy and selfish ambition in your hearts, do not boast about it or deny the truth."*
James 3:14

Now, there is also an earthly wisdom that we want to stay away from. It is the wisdom that says, "I am number one and I need to promote me!" You see that kind of wisdom in the business world, in sports and even at your school. What are the characteristics of this kind of wisdom?

There is bitter envy which means, "You don't deserve what you have" or "I want what you have." This leads to gossip and an attempt on your part to bring the other person down so that you can look better or get what they have. The bitter part says, "I hate you, I can't stand you and I despise you." It causes you to become hard on the inside. You lose sensitivity to what is right and wrong so you can't even see that what you're doing is totally wrong. You justify your actions in your mind and to your friends because you think the other person deserves this kind of behavior. Here are some verses on envy that I want you to study. Write down what God is saying to you in these verses: 1 Corinthians 13:4, Galatians 5:21 and Philippians 1:15-17.

There is also an aspect of envy that says, "I want what you have so I will follow your behavior." Look at these two verses:

Proverbs 3:31: *"Do not envy a violent man or choose any of his ways, for the Lord detests a perverse man but takes the upright into his confidence."*

Proverbs 23:17: *"Do not let your heart envy sinners, but always be zealous for the fear of the Lord."*

If you envy the violent man or the sinner, you are likely to follow their examples. Don't do that because God detests these kinds of people.

Next there is selfish ambition, which means, "I am getting to the top no matter who I have to step on or hurt. I want what I want and I don't really care about others."

You want to rally people to your side and you cause dissention, division and cliques within your youth group and school. You want to be acknowledged, recognized and honored. You want to be seen as the leader and the most spiritual. You oppose anyone you think is in the way of getting what you want and that includes your Youth Pastor, Senior Pastor, parents, teachers, peers, boss, etc. You are more concerned with yourself than with Jesus Christ. You have a false humility that acts humble on the outside but your heart is far from God.

This person loves to argue, quarrel and debate about a lot of different things. They always need to be right and they are not teachable because they think they already know everything. Study these verses and tell me what the Lord is saying to you: Proverbs 17:19, Proverbs 20:3, Proverbs 26:21, Philippians 2:3-4, 2 Timothy 2:14 and 2 Timothy 2:24.

The third part of earthly wisdom is boasting. Pride loves to boast, "Look at me, look at everything I have done, look at how talented I am, how pretty I am and how incredibly humble I am." You see this kind of boasting in the lives of the rich and famous, but sadly you also see it in some "Christian" celebrities. I have been with musicians and speakers who are in love with themselves. Their favorite stories are about them and they have little interest about anything else. They boast about where they have been and what they have done. Their boasting is very open and in your face.

There are also individuals that look humble on the outside, but have hearts that boast. They are secretly happy when someone fails. They like to receive recognition and they want to be better than those around them. These people are more concerned about themselves than the cause of Christ. You can see that in their priorities--what they spend their time pursuing, thinking about and doing. Here are some verses to study. Think about what God is saying to you: Proverbs 11:2, Proverbs 27:1, Matthew 23:12, Romans 12:16 and 1 John 2:16.

The fourth part of earthly wisdom is denying the truth. Before I came to Christ, I was a Christian Scientist and grew up in a cult. When I came to Christ, I would sit down and talk to my grandmother, who was still a staunch Christian Scientist. We would talk about God, faith and truth. I would show her the contradictions between what Christian Science said and what the Bible said and she would give me a hard time by saying, "I have already made up my mind so don't confuse me with the facts." At over ninety years of age, my grandmother gave her heart to Jesus Christ and stepped from darkness into light. Before she died, she said to me, "I think of all the years that I wasted." **We end up wasting our lives when we deny the truth and follow lies.**

You deny the truth when you seek after the things of the world. You deny the truth when you allow the enemy to deceive you into believing that the world will fulfill you more than Jesus will. You deny the truth when you preach one thing and live another.
We call these people hypocrites and we are all guilty of that to one extent or another.

Jesus Christ promised that if you know the truth, the truth will set you free. To deny the truth is to live in bondage. We end up living in bondage to sin, self-hate, boy/girlfriends, food, others, etc. The truth is the Word of God and the key is not merely understanding it, but living it out day by day.

Some of the saddest and most miserable teenagers I meet are those that know the truth, but are choosing to live in sin. These students move in the opposite direction of what they know is right and true. They're just like the prodigal son and I always pray that they will soon come to their senses and come back to the Father.

Bitter envy, selfish ambition, boasting and denying the truth are all part of what the world sees as wisdom. Promoting myself and getting to the top no matter what I have to do or whom I have to hurt. Earthly wisdom is all about rationalizing, making excuses and not taking responsibility. It is all about what makes me happy, what I want and what makes me look good. To follow this kind of wisdom is to deny the truth and you WILL be miserable.

## SOMETHING TO THINK ABOUT:

1. Do you see any earthly wisdom in your life?

2. I believe you know what is true, but are you living the truth?

3. You will never feel worse than when you know what you ought to be doing, but choose not to do it.

## SOMETHING TO PRAY ABOUT:

Pray that God would reveal any earthly wisdom that is in your life. Ask Him to show you if there are any areas where you have been denying the truth.

## USE THIS SPACE TO JOURNAL ABOUT WHAT GOD IS SAYING TO YOU:

# DAY FIFTY-EIGHT – JAMES 3:15

## SOMETHING TO STUDY:

*"Such 'wisdom' does not come down from heaven but is earthly,*
*unspiritual, of the devil."*
James 3:15

The wisdom that we just talked about yesterday is not the kind of wisdom that you ought to be seeking. Envy, selfish ambition, boasting and denying the truth do not come down from heaven. You never need to pray and ask God, "Is it your will that I be envious?" The answer will always be, "No!" The earthly wisdom that we are talking about falls into three categories:

- Earthly

This wisdom is earthly and the world uses it to get ahead. Earthly wisdom is all about becoming rich and famous and getting a lot of stuff. It's about having a big house, nice car, large boat, beautiful vacation home and other people to do what you don't want to do. When you are young, this all sounds very, very good. But as you get older, you will see how shallow and empty this kind of wisdom holds. Have you seen the bumper sticker that says, "Whoever dies with the most toys wins?" How wrong is that kind of thinking? This is what earthly wisdom believes. Get all you can so that in the end you can win and be the best. What good do all the awards in the world do once you die and enter eternity?

- Unspiritual

Second, such wisdom is unspiritual and not of God. Have you heard evangelists and pastors that talk about naming it and claiming it? They believe that if you have faith, God's desire is to make you rich. You should be driving big cars, living in big houses and having big bank accounts. This is sick and wrong. Are they saying that our brothers and sisters in third world countries don't have faith? I want to suggest it is just the opposite, those men and women in countries of great poverty or persecution have faith that would put those "name it-claim it" preachers to shame.

Don't get me wrong, I am not saying that being wealthy is unspiritual. I know Godly men and women who have been given a lot of money and they use it to the glory of God. I am saying that it is wrong to claim that if you only had more faith you would have a lot of money. I oppose the TV evangelist that tells you to give a lot of money to them so that God will give a lot of money to you. These people boast, have selfish ambition, envy and deny the truth. Don't support them or follow after them. If your pastor is one of those "name it-claim it" people, then run, don't walk, and get out of that church.

- Of the devil

Finally, this wisdom is of the devil. Earthly wisdom is inspired by Satan himself and he uses it to deceive and lead people astray. Does it concern you that some preachers today are following after the devil? It does me and I want to make sure that I am not seeking the wisdom of this world. What about you?

## SOMETHING TO THINK ABOUT:

1. You only want to sit under the ministry of someone that teaches and pursues Godly wisdom.

2. **Not everyone who calls on the Lord knows the Lord**.

3. How important are the things of this world to you?

## SOMETHING TO PRAY ABOUT:

Ask God to give you His wisdom so that you can discern the truth from lies. Tell Him that you don't want anything to do with earthly wisdom.

## USE THIS SPACE TO JOURNAL ABOUT WHAT GOD IS SAYING TO YOU:

# DAY FIFTY-NINE – JAMES 3:16

## SOMETHING TO STUDY:

*"For where you have envy and selfish ambition, there you find disorder and every evil practice."*
James 3:16

If you decide to buy into the world and its values, if you seek after earthly wisdom, then you need to understand that there are consequences to your choices. The first consequence is disorder. Things don't work out the way you wanted them to or thought they would. Plans fall through, relationships are broken and life becomes very confused. What does this lead to inside your life? You become angry, depressed, fearful and desperate. You begin to move further and further away from God. Instead of turning from the earthly wisdom and seeking after God, you just try harder to get what you want. You become more envious and self-seeking.

This leads to the second consequence--every evil practice. You say to me, "I am not involved in every evil practice." But are you headed in that direction? You must understand that one sin leads to another. **Evil never stays static; it always increases and gets worse unless you do something to stop it.** Here are two passages I want you to read and think about: Romans 1:28-32 and 2 Timothy 3:1-5. Here is a list of evil practices: Wickedness, evil, greed, depravity, envy, murder, strife, deceit, malice, gossip, God-haters, insolent, arrogant, boastful, invent ways of doing evil, disobey their parents, senseless, faithless, heartless, ruthless, lover of themselves, lover of money, proud, abusive, ungrateful, unholy, without love, unforgiving, slanderous, without self-control, brutal, not lovers of the good, treacherous, rash, conceited, lovers of pleasure rather than lovers of God--having a form of godliness but denying its power.

How many of these evil practices are you involved in right now? Earthly wisdom is a slippery slope that will drag you down. You don't jump into this evil all at once. The enemy is smarter than that and has plenty of time so he brings you down one step at a time. He leads you from one evil practice to another. He helps you to rationalize and excuse the actions in your mind so he can take you deeper and deeper. I want to grab you by the shoulders, shake you very hard and yell this into your face, "WAKE UP!"

163

Check out Romans 13:11-14, *"And do this, understanding the present time. The hour has come for you to wake up from your slumber, because our salvation is nearer now than when we first believed. The night is nearly over; the day is almost here. So let us put aside the deeds of darkness and put on the armor of light. Let us behave decently, as in the daytime, not in orgies and drunkenness, not in sexual immorality and debauchery, not in dissension and jealousy. Rather, clothe yourselves with the Lord Jesus Christ, and do not think about how to gratify the desires of the sinful nature."*

It is not too late, but you must turn back to God and receive His forgiveness, mercy and grace. You can be different because God will give you the power.

## SOMETHING TO THINK ABOUT:

1. Are there evil practices and disorder in your life?

2. What do you need to do today in your relationship with Christ?

3. God will keep you from sin or sin will keep you from God.

## SOMETHING TO PRAY ABOUT:

Ask God to keep you from all evil practices, confess any sin and live for Jesus.

## USE THIS SPACE TO JOURNAL ABOUT WHAT GOD IS SAYING TO YOU:

# DAY SIXTY – JAMES 3:17a

## SOMETHING TO STUDY:

*"But the wisdom that comes from heaven is first of all pure; then*
*peace-loving, considerate, submissive…"*
James 3:17a

We are called to stay away from the earth's wisdom because that will get us into a lot of trouble. In its place, we will pursue the wisdom that comes from heaven. The source of this heavenly wisdom is God and it is available to you just by asking. When you ask, you will receive and then you will begin to see the truth and know the truth. As you live out this heavenly wisdom, you will be radically changed. What are the results of asking for God's wisdom? There are eight wonderful, positive, life-giving results. Let's start by looking at the first four.

First, **God's wisdom is pure**. Pure thoughts and pure actions; that means you have no ulterior motives, no envy, no selfish ambition, no boasting or denying the truth. You become a God seeker and a God pleaser. God will give you a desire to live a clean and pure life.

Rest in His arms and know that He has made you pure. Take your wonderful Bible and turn to Colossians 1:22 and read it. What does it say to you? It says that God the Father has made you right in His sight because of Jesus Christ's death on the cross for your sins. Now He is presenting you holy, without blemish and free from accusation. You don't have to become holy and pure; you are already holy and pure. So live like it and don't defile all the good things that God has done in your life.

His desire is that you would stay pure on the inside. That means you don't defile yourself by taking garbage into your life. Remember, if you take garbage into your life, garbage is what comes out of your life. What do you need to get rid of in order to remain pure on the inside? Let me give you some suggestions: pornography, smoking, drugs, drinking, overeating, starving yourself, cutting, and some of the music, movies, TV programs, DVD's, magazines and books that you are into. Ask the Holy Spirit and He will tell you exactly what you need to get rid of so that you can be pure on the inside.

Your relationships need to be pure. **Show me who you hang around with and I will show you the kind of person that you are becoming.** 1 Corinthians 15:33 says, *"Do not be misled: Bad company corrupts good character."* Your relationships are either building you up or pulling you down. They either draw you closer to Christ or push you further away. My encouragement to you is the next verse, *"Come back to your senses as you ought, and stop sinning; for there are some who are ignorant of God-I say this to your shame."* Make sure your relationships are pure. There are a lot of good reasons for this, but the number one reason is so that your friends will find Christ and live for Him.

You always want to strive to keep your conscience clear before God and man (Acts 24:16). That means making choices that you don't have to feel guilty about or regret later on. I tell students, "Don't do something today that you will regret tomorrow."

Second, **heavenly wisdom is peace-loving**. "Do not be anxious about anything, but in everything, by prayer and petition, with thanksgiving, present your requests to God. And the peace of God, which transcends all understanding, will guard your hearts and your minds in Christ Jesus" (Philippians 4:6-7). You will experience an inward peace as you seek God and His will for your life. That sense of comfort and security is in knowing that God is still on the throne, He is in control and you can trust Him. The result is that you don't have to be worried about anything.

You will also have peace with your neighbors; you can give a blessing in response to an insult. You want to be kind, sensitive and loving toward others, but it is not a peace-at-all-costs kind of attitude. Stand against lies, evil, bad theology and sin; confront lovingly, even though this may lead to conflict with the other person. You must always love others enough to risk your relationships with them because you desire what is very best for them. Here are some great verses on peace: John 14:27, John 16:33, Romans 12:18, Romans 14:19, Colossians 3:15-17, 2 Thessalonians 3:16 and Hebrews 13:20-21.

Third, **heavenly wisdom is considerate**. Being considerate to those around you is love in action. I am amazed at how many people are totally clueless and inconsiderate. They live in their own little worlds and they are their own gods. They don't care if they are loud, if their kids are out of control or if they are bothering others. Be considerate; that means putting your love into action. Look around, notice the needs of others and do something. Being considerate motivates you to action...

- Always leave a place looking better than when you arrived.
- Look for chances to serve other people.
- When God points out a need, seek to meet it immediately.
- Feed the hungry, clothe the naked, care for the widow and play with the fatherless.
- Be a listener.
- Rejoice with those who rejoice and weep with those who weep.

Fourth, **heavenly wisdom is being submissive**. We all have weaknesses and areas that need improvement. Are you willing to make yourself accountable and look for opportunities to be sharpened by others? Being submissive means that you are open to learning the lessons that God wants to teach you. He can speak to you through His Word, prayer and others. Are you listening?

Being submissive also means that you are learning to be obedient-- obedient to your parents and those in authority over you, like your teachers. God is not going to honor you as a leader until you have learned to be a follower. How can you expect others to follow you when you are not willing to follow others? Joshua was obedient to Moses and sat at his feet to learn before God made him leader of the children of Israel.

Obedience is not a dirty word and it is not a weakness. It takes tremendous strength to be obedient and to follow someone else's leadership. It takes heavenly wisdom and someone who is submissive.

## SOMETHING TO THINK ABOUT:

1. Don't put off until tomorrow what you can do today!

2. Are you teachable?

3. God has made you holy, are you living like you are holy?

## SOMETHING TO PRAY ABOUT:

Tell God that you want His wisdom. Pray that you would be pure, peace-loving, considerate and submissive. Ask Him to give you the opportunities to put these characteristics into practice.

## USE THIS SPACE TO JOURNAL ABOUT WHAT GOD IS SAYING TO YOU:

# DAY SIXTY-ONE – JAMES 3:17b

## SOMETHING TO STUDY:

> *"... full of mercy and good fruit, impartial and sincere."*
> James 3:17b

Yesterday we looked at the first four results of seeking Godly wisdom. Now we are going to check out the next four. As you are seeking after the Lord, this is what He will be producing in your life.

Fifth, **heavenly wisdom is being full of mercy**. You don't seek to get revenge or get even. You are able to forgive because you are greatly forgiven. God has given us what we don't deserve. What we deserve is judgment and condemnation, but He doesn't give us what we deserve and that my friend is mercy. Receiving mercy should humble us and cause us to be so grateful. We should want to treat others the way Christ treats us. By doing so we become a living and breathing example of Jesus Christ to our friends and neighbors. One indication of mercy is giving to someone who can't return the favor. You are setting them free from a debt they owe or a wrong they have done. Mercy is giving someone a wonderful blessing.

Sixth, **heavenly wisdom produces good fruit**. You are producing fruit whether you like it or not. You can produce good fruit or you can produce bad fruit. Heavenly wisdom produces good fruit and earthly wisdom produces bad fruit. Am I going too fast for you? Good fruit seeks to meet the needs of others while bad fruit is self-seeking. When you are producing good fruit, you are motivated to action. You can read more about the fruit of the Spirit in Galatians 5:22-23.

Seventh, **heavenly wisdom is being impartial**. God is not partial, and freely gives wisdom to whoever asks. You don't have to be rich, good-looking, popular or smart; all you need is a personal relationship with Jesus Christ and faith to receive the wisdom. Remember that **wisdom is seeing life through the eyes of God** --to want what God wants, to be what He wants you to be, to go where He wants you to go and to respond the way He wants you to respond.

Being impartial also means you are not to show favoritism. It is okay to have best friends, but not to the exclusion of others. Everyone should feel welcomed and loved when they are around you.

Finally, **heavenly wisdom is sincere**. That means it is free from being fake, phony and hypocritical. You live what you believe and allow people to see the real you. You are not one way at school and another at church. You're not trying to purposely deceive people and you aren't living a lie.

If you are full of mercy, with good fruit, impartial and sincere then good job!

## SOMETHING TO THINK ABOUT:

1. Are you showing mercy? Are you forgiving and understanding?

2. Have you asked for wisdom today?

3. If you are sincere, you have let down the masks.

## SOMETHING TO PRAY ABOUT:

Ask God to give you mercy today in all situations. When you are behind the wheel of the car, shopping, at school or at home, ask God for wisdom so that you can see life through His eyes.

## USE THIS SPACE TO JOURNAL ABOUT WHAT GOD IS SAYING TO YOU:

# DAY SIXTY-TWO – JAMES 3:18

## SOMETHING TO STUDY:

*"Peacemakers who sow in peace raise a harvest of righteousness."*
James 3:18

If you sow beans, you don't harvest corn and if you sow anger, you don't harvest righteousness. If you want to end up in the right place, then you need to start at the right point. What are you sowing into the people around you? If it's anger and self-centeredness, then you will reap discord, cliques and conflict. Some of your lives are filled with all kinds of problems. Ask yourself the question, "What am I sowing into my life and those around me?"

A harvest of righteousness begins with peace. First and foremost is a peace with God, which means I am living correctly and in a way that pleases God and brings a smile to His face. We never want to be in a place of opposition to God because that will reap the opposite of righteousness. Sin, death and destruction await those who live in opposition to God. They experience a lot of things that the world has to offer, but miss out on the righteous life that pleases God.

Next, we must be at peace with others. "I love mankind; it's people I can't stand." I don't know who first said that, but I can relate. People drive me crazy! I sit here in Starbucks, my office, and I look out into the parking lot. When the lot is full, people pull into the handicap parking space even though they are not handicapped. That makes me mad. I am waiting in line and a woman cuts in front of me because she is in a hurry and that makes me mad. People drive like idiots and that makes me mad. I pull up to a stop sign and there is a car to my left signaling to make a left hand turn, I am making a right hand turn. I start to go and my daughter screams because the person in the left hand lane decides to turn right and that makes me mad. God says, "Greg, if you are going to harvest righteousness in your life and in those around you, then you need to understand and forgive." We must see people from God's perspective and not just the way they are at the moment. We need to see what they could become if they just committed their lives to Jesus Christ.

Finally, you need to be at peace with yourself. If you don't like yourself or the choices you are making, you will not experience peace.

171

**To experience peace you must see yourself through the eyes of God and know that you are His special creation, made in His image and loved deeply.** You must also live according to your beliefs and morals, because if you don't, you will experience chaos and self-hate. To be a hypocrite is to be a miserable and guilty person.

If you live at peace with God, others and you, then you will harvest a life of righteousness and that is a life worth living!

## SOMETHING TO THINK ABOUT:

1. What have you been sowing?

2. What is harder for you, being at peace with God, others or yourself?

3. Sow peace and reap righteousness or sow anger and reap conflict, you make the choice.

## SOMETHING TO PRAY ABOUT:

Ask God to give you the strength and power to sow in peace, to be kind to those around you and to be in a right relationship with Him. Tell Him that you want to harvest righteousness.

## USE THIS SPACE TO JOURNAL ABOUT WHAT GOD IS SAYING TO YOU:

# DAY SIXTY-THREE – JAMES 4:1

## SOMETHING TO STUDY:

*"What causes fights and quarrels among you? Don't they come from your desires that battle within you?"*
James 4:1

James starts off the fourth chapter with a pretty amazing statement; uncontrolled passions and desires are responsible for all the fights and quarrels experienced here on earth. Whether it's between neighbors or nations, fights occur because someone desires something like money, land, respect or understanding and they don't get it. In their minds, people start scheming to get what they want; the scheming might take months or only moments. Then one day or the next moment those desires become action. People end up doing whatever they need to do to get what they desire. This can lead to arguments or even physical confrontation leading to wars.

What causes quarrels and fights in the church and youth group? The answer is the desires and passions that battle within you. Those desires lead to broken friendships, cliques and split churches.

**Notice that the real battle is happening inside your life.** The battle is between your old nature that desires to be selfish and self-centered and your new nature that desires to please Jesus and live for Him. When a church splits, answer me this question, has the new nature or the old nature won? Do you think it is God's desire and will that a church should split? What kind of example is that to the world and the non-Christian? I see individuals and couples that are constantly jumping from church to church because they don't like something the pastor said or did. So if they can't get their way, they leave. Now, I understand that there are legitimate reasons for leaving a church, but many times it has to do with selfish desires. The problem is that no one will admit that they left because they are selfish.

If you are not careful, you will begin to listen to your desires more than you listen to God. You will stop praying and end up turning your back on the Holy Spirit. This leads to all the conflict and problems that you are having. The desires that you have are not necessarily bad. You desire food, water, love, God and this book and that is all very good! The problems come when your desires are out of the control of the Holy Spirit.

What causes quarrels and fights in your life and circle of friends? Aren't they the desires that are inside your life? Why don't you get along with your parents? Isn't it because you desire something that they won't let you do or have? Get your eyes off of everyone else and stop making excuses. What changes do you need to make in your life?

## SOMETHING TO THINK ABOUT:

1. Who is in control of your desires?

2. What is causing fights and quarrels in your youth group?

3. YOU are a selfish person and need the Holy Spirit in control of your life!

## SOMETHING TO PRAY ABOUT:

Surrender your desires to the Lord of Lords. Tell Him that you want to desire what He wants for you. Ask Him to reveal your selfishness to you.

## USE THIS SPACE TO JOURNAL ABOUT WHAT GOD IS SAYING TO YOU:

# DAY SIXTY-FOUR – JAMES 4:2

## SOMETHING TO STUDY:

*"You want something but don't get it. You kill and covet, but you cannot have what you want. You quarrel and fight. You do not have, because you do not ask God."*
James 4:2

What is the bottom line of this verse? What is the major problem? We don't trust God. We do not believe that He will meet our needs or take care of us. Notice it says, "You do not have, because you do not ask God." For many of us, God is our last resort rather than our first thought. After we have tried everything ourselves and worked our hardest to get what we want, then we might turn to God in desperation for help.

God knows you better than you know yourself and He understands your deepest needs and desires. **You can trust Him to take care of you.** If you do, then you will save yourself a lot of trouble and conflict.

Because we don't trust God, we begin to take these steps:

- You want something. Maybe it is good for you, maybe it isn't. Maybe you really need it, maybe you don't. For one reason or another, you don't get it. So, instead of seeking the Lord and trusting Him with every detail of your life, you decide to take matters into your own hands and you take step two.

- You kill and covet. I hear what you are saying, "I have never killed nor would I kill." Please read Matthew 5:21-22 and tell me what it is saying to you. Here is what it says to me, if I kill someone then I am subject to judgment. But if I am angry with my brother, then I am also under judgment. You have never killed someone, but have you been angry with someone because of those desires working inside your life? This step is happening inside of you or behind the back of the person that you're upset with. You seek to kill them emotionally and destroy them as a person by gossiping and being critical of them to others. At the same

175

time, you covet and want what they have or what they won't let you have.

- You quarrel and fight. In other words, you come into direct conflict with another person. You end up saying and doing things that you end up regretting.

It is always better to ask of God and trust Him. He will take care of you and give you what you really need. Who knows what is better for you, you or God? Stop fighting with Him and accept the fact that God will say no to some things that you really want because it will hurt you in the long run. It is always better to ask God and trust Him rather than get into all kinds of conflict with those around you.

## SOMETHING TO THINK ABOUT:

1. Ask God first and if you really need it, He will supply.

2. Is God your first thought or your last resort when you want something?

3. Do you get angry, covet, quarrel and fight much? How much?

## SOMETHING TO PRAY ABOUT:

Ask God for what you want and desire. Thank Him that He always answers prayer and be willing to accept what God knows is best for you.

## USE THIS SPACE TO JOURNAL ABOUT WHAT GOD IS SAYING TO YOU:

# DAY SIXTY-FIVE – JAMES 4:3

## SOMETHING TO STUDY:

*"When you ask, you do not receive, because you ask with wrong motives, that you may spend what you get on your pleasures."*
James 4:3

It is important to discern the difference between wants and needs. If you don't know the difference, the good news is that God sees the difference and He will help if you let Him.

God always answers prayer and I believe that He answers in one of three ways:

- **Yes**-good request, here is the answer. God delights in giving to His children and He desires to say yes to our requests, but He also knows what is best for us.

- **No**-bad request, I am not going to give you what you want. We don't like it, but no is an answer. He knows what is best for you, so there will be times when He says no because the request will hurt you or someone else in the long run.

- **Grow**-good request, bad timing. God desires to answer this request, but not at this moment. Maybe you are asking for someone special to come into your life. The Lord will do that, but first you need to grow more spiritually so you don't end up compromising. Maybe you are praying for a family member's healing. The Lord is going to do that, but first He wants to teach them something through the pain. **Remember that God's delays are not necessarily His denials.** Be patient because God wants to see you and others grow and mature as Godly men and women.

The problem is that you want God to will what you want rather than wanting what God wills. You don't receive what you ask because your motive is so bad. You want things that will bring you pleasure. You are self-centered and you need to be Christ-centered. Instead of being thankful for everything you have, you end up complaining about what you don't have. You will fall into this never-ending negative cycle and you are never satisfied. "I want…I want…I want…nicer clothes, more money, less weight, newer car, better sound system," and on…and on…and on it goes. You are looking for this "thing" to make you happy and fulfilled, but the real need is inside your life and your heart. Nothing on the outside will make you as happy as Jesus will when you trust Him completely. You don't need stuff, boy/girlfriend, recognition, power and control…you need Jesus!

When you are satisfied and thankful for what you have, that will lead to contentment. Because it comes from God, contentment produces a peace that passes all understanding and opens your life to the blessing of the Lord. When you are satisfied, you are saying, "God I trust you to take care of me."

## SOMETHING TO THINK ABOUT:

1. God always answers prayer. Do you believe that is true?

2. Jesus will give you more than the world could even begin to supply.

3. What would happen if you completely surrendered to Jesus Christ?

## SOMETHING TO PRAY ABOUT:

Tell Jesus that you want Him more than anything. Tell Him that you love Him and you will trust Him to supply all your needs.

## USE THIS SPACE TO JOURNAL ABOUT WHAT GOD IS SAYING TO YOU:

# DAY SIXTY-SIX – JAMES 4:4

## SOMETHING TO STUDY:

*"You adulterous people, don't you know that friendship with the world is hatred toward God? Anyone who chooses to be a friend of the world becomes an enemy of God."*
James 4:4

This is very strong and convicting; God isn't beating around the bush. I appreciate that the Lord speaks the truth and doesn't pull any punches. You are adulterous if you have forsaken your first love, Jesus Christ. Grab your Bible and turn to the book of Revelation and read chapter 2, verses 1-5. John starts off by complimenting the church in Ephesus and recognizing that they have been doing some things really well. Then in verse four he says, *"Yet I hold this against you: You have forsaken your first love."* Who was their first love? It was Jesus Christ and they turned away to other things. Have you forgotten Jesus and turned to other things and people? Then you too have become adulterous.

Would you tolerate a person that said to you, "I want to marry you, but I also want to be able to sleep around after we are married and I want you to stick with me and continue to love me?" I am hoping that you would say, "Kiss off!" But we end up treating Jesus this way when we say, "Jesus, I love you and want to spend eternity with you, but I also want the things of the world. So, I will be sinning and messing around, but I still want you to love me." We should be very surprised that Jesus doesn't tell us to kiss off.

What do we need to do? Go back to Revelation chapter 2 and check out the first part of verse 5, *"Remember the height from which you have fallen! Repent and do the things you did at first."* So, first of all acknowledge that you have fallen and fallen quite a bit. Think back to when you and Jesus were best friends and the things that you used to do. Now, whether you feel like it or not, begin to do those things again. Get back into the Word of God, pray, hang with Christian friends, share your faith, get back to church, worship, be obedient, etc. In other words, get back to your first love!

Friendship with the world means that you are not only committing adultery, but you are also telling God that you hate Him. I realize that you don't mean to do this, but this is why it is so important that you stop being friends with the world. Take your Bible; you still have it, don't you? Take the Bible and turn to 1 Corinthians 6:19-20 and read what it says, *"...You are not your own; you were bought at a price. Therefore honor God with your body."* You aren't just married to Christ; you belong to Him like a slave belongs to his master. You have no right to go into the world and seek to be its friend. You have run away from your master and He has a right to kill you, to reject you and to cast you from His sight and into hell. Why should He put up with someone that takes His death on the cross for granted? Why should He put up with someone that spits in His face and drags Him through all the sin of the world? Why should He put up with someone who wants to be a friend of the world?

To be friends with the world is to become an enemy of God. That is not a good position to be in at any time of your life. What do you think of when you see someone as your enemy?

- You can't trust them.
- They are against you.
- You want to beat them.
- They disgust you.
- You have intense feelings against them.
- They are to be avoided.

Is this how you want God to view you? No, I am pretty sure you never want to be an enemy of God. You are setting yourself up to lose big time.

What if God acted, reacted and dealt with people the way we do? He would eternally reject us. However, we can be thankful that God is God and not Greg Speck because He says, "Let everyone else be unfaithful but I am faithful." (2 Timothy 2:13) God also says, "...Never will I leave you; never will I forsake you," in Hebrews 13:5b.

Wouldn't it be great if we were as committed to Jesus Christ as He is committed to us? Well, we can be, if we are willing to make some tough choices. All of life is filled with choices; I will do this or I won't do that.

Who will be your friend, Jesus Christ or the world? This is a decision that only you can make. What are some characteristics of being a good friend?

- You spend time with them.
- They do some of the same things you do.
- You trust and confide in them.
- They are proud of you and acknowledge you before others.
- You love them.

Can you see why you need to choose one or the other? How can you claim to love Jesus when you are a friend of the world? **Jesus Christ is either Lord of all or He isn't Lord at all.** Either He is worthy of your life and love or He isn't. If you choose to be a friend of the world, then you choose to be an enemy of God and say that you hate Him.

Turn in your Bible to Joshua 24:14-15 and underline this passage. It is a favorite passage of Scripture for me and it says, *"Now fear the Lord and serve him with all faithfulness. Throw away the gods your forefathers worshiped beyond the River and in Egypt, and serve the Lord. But if serving the Lord seems undesirable to you, then choose for yourselves this day whom you will serve, whether the gods your forefathers served beyond the River, or the gods of the Amorites, in whose land you are living. But as for me and my household, we will serve the Lord."*

As for Greg Speck and his family, we will serve the Lord. What about you? *"All the nations may walk in the name of their gods; we will walk in the name of the Lord our God forever and ever,"* (Micah 4:5). Are you willing to make that commitment and take that stand? What would you need to start doing and what would you need to stop doing?

Following Jesus Christ has never been easy; it is not the path of cowards. To follow Jesus Christ means to love Him with all your heart, mind, soul and strength. It means you will no longer be friends with the world and you will be faithful to your first love...Jesus!

## SOMETHING TO THINK ABOUT:

1. Choose this day who you will serve!

2. What is so appealing about the world that you would sacrifice your relationship with Jesus Christ?

3. Treat Jesus better than you would treat a close friend.

## SOMETHING TO PRAY ABOUT:

Tell God that you want to love and serve Him. Tell Him that you never want to be His enemy. Ask Him to forgive you for the times you have been unfaithful to Him. Thank Him for always being faithful to you!

## USE THIS SPACE TO JOURNAL ABOUT WHAT GOD IS SAYING TO YOU:

# DAY SIXTY-SEVEN – JAMES 4:5

## SOMETHING TO STUDY:

*"Or do you think Scripture says without reason that the spirit he caused to live in us envies intensely?"*
James 4:5

What does this verse mean? Before you read any further think about it and tell the Lord what you think it is saying to you. Now let's see if you and I agree.

Did you know that God is a jealous God? Here are some verses that I would like you to read: Exodus 20:5-6, Deuteronomy 4:24 and Joshua 24:19. Now look at what Paul says in 2 Corinthians 11:2-3, *"I am jealous for you with a godly jealousy. I promised you to one husband, to Christ, so that I might present you as a pure virgin to him. But I am afraid that just as Eve was deceived by the serpent's cunning, your minds may somehow be led astray from your sincere and pure devotion to Christ."*

We have talked about the evil side of jealousy and envy. However, these verses are showing us that there is also a good side. God and Paul are jealous for our best and don't want us to settle for anything less than His very best for our lives. God doesn't want to see us following the world because He knows the pain and temptation that we will face. The Holy Spirit, who lives within us, also envies intensely for our good. He wants us to know the joy, peace and love of following Christ with our whole hearts. He doesn't want to see us make bad choices and get hurt.

During one of my speaking engagements, I meet a girl that was going home to become part of a cult because the boy she liked was in the cult. I talked to her, her parents talked to her and other Godly men and women talked to her, but she would not listen to anyone. I told her that she was setting herself up for a lot of pain, but she didn't care because she liked this guy. She was moving out of her house and into his house to become a cult member. I recently received this note from her. I know it is long, but let it be a warning to all of us who are tempted to walk away from God and not listen to Godly instruction.

"It has been a long time since I have talked to you. A lot has happened. I have been on a long and painful journey. I will start from the last time I talked to you, which was my senior year. I lived with the cult family but I didn't like it but it allowed me to see what this cult really believed. I realized that the differences between the cult and Christianity were huge. So I moved away from the family but I also decided to move away from God and started partying and having sex. I hated my life and tried to commit suicide two times. Once I OD'ed on "over the counter" medicine and the next time I slit my wrists. I went back and visited my parents for two weeks and realized that I needed to change but I didn't want to give up my lifestyle. After I returned home from visiting my parents I got alcohol poisoning, my car was broken into and later it was stolen. My driver's license was suspended and I had an unpaid ticket. Life went from bad to worse, I became addicted to marijuana and tried to commit suicide again, this time it was more serious. I was living with my boyfriend and he found me unconscious. I told my parents what had happened and they suggested that I get help so I started seeing a Christian psychologist and he diagnosed me as being clinically depressed. I lost my job and a friend got me a job in a massage parlor. I was giving illegal massages to men and ended up becoming a prostitute. I finally quit the job when I discovered that I was pregnant. I called and told my parents that I was pregnant and they said they would love and support me no matter what happened. I knew right then that I couldn't get an abortion. I was not sure who the father was and I am still not sure. I have now moved back with my parents and recently discovered that I am going to have twins, a boy and a girl. I have finally come back to the Lord. It has been very hard to change because of everything I have been through. I now have an accountability partner that I meet with once a week, plus my Dad and I go out to breakfast once a week. That has helped a lot. I am trying to read the Bible everyday and I am also reading a book on purity."

Do you think this was God's desire for her life? No, He is jealous for our good. He wants what is best for us. God didn't want her to go through these painful things. God's desire was that she would live for Him and not the world. Please learn from her mistakes and make good choices. He gives us the awesome privilege and responsibility of choice. We can choose to follow Him or we can choose to walk away. What will you do?

Notice how the sin progressed? She didn't go home and immediately become a prostitute. The enemy is very shrewd and has you make bad choices, one step at a time, pulling you deeper and deeper into sin.

- Rebels against her parents.
- Doesn't listen to Godly counsel.
- Moves toward a Cult, a false religion with false gods, opening herself up to the deception and lies of Satan.
- Starts partying and having sex.
- Tries to commit suicide three times.
- Becomes involved with drugs.
- Works illegally in a massage parlor, which leads her to become a prostitute.

The Holy Spirit is intensely envious that you do not go through what this girl went through. What is the difference between good envy and bad envy? Bad envy says, "I want what you have and I don't think you deserve to have it." Good envy says, "I want to see you do well and not settle for anything less than God's very best for your life."

Are you moving in the right direction? You need to choose between what is easy and what is right. Sin is easy, but God is calling you to do what is right and pleasing in His sight. Nothing is better or more fulfilling than becoming everything that Jesus Christ has created you to be. Listen to the Holy Spirit within you and to Godly counsel. Move in the direction that will build you up and bring honor to God. You live to glorify the King, why would you want anything else?

## SOMETHING TO THINK ABOUT:

1. Can you learn from the mistakes of others or do you need to learn about life the hard way? Are you heading in the same direction that this girl was heading?

2. What is the difference between good envy and bad envy?

3. Why would you want anything less than God's best?

## SOMETHING TO PRAY ABOUT:

Thank the Holy Spirit that He intensely envies for your best. Tell Him that you will listen and be obedient to what He wants you to do.

## USE THIS SPACE TO JOURNAL ABOUT WHAT GOD IS SAYING TO YOU:

# DAY SIXTY-EIGHT – JAMES 4:6

## SOMETHING TO STUDY:

*"But he gives us more grace. That is why Scripture says: 'God opposes the proud but gives grace to the humble'."*
James 4:6

What a great promise this verse is for us today! God gives us grace and more grace. Grace is His favor and blessing upon your life. It is all about His perfect timing in meeting your needs. Today God wants to pour out His grace on your life! You are His child and you are deeply loved, not because of what you do, but because of who you are. All you need to do is humble yourself and be willing to receive this grace.

Hebrews 4:16 says, *"Let us approach the throne of grace with confidence, so that we may receive mercy and find grace to help us in our time of need."* Picture Jesus Christ stepping down from his throne, standing before you with His arms open wide and inviting you to run to Him. Run to Him so that He can bless, protect and love you. Are you willing to do that right now? Are you willing to receive His grace, His blessing and His favor on your life? Who wouldn't want something like that?

But the promise comes with a warning and it is something that you and I have talked about before. God opposes the proud. Pretty simple and straightforward, but it's not always easy for us to see it in our own life. Do you struggle with pride?

- Will you allow others to help you?
- Are you open about your struggles?
- Do you listen to Godly advice?
- Are you teachable?
- Do you obey your parents?
- Do you always have to be right and win every argument?
- Are you telling stories that always make you look great?
- Do you spend most of your time talking about yourself?
- Are you always saying, "I know," when people try to tell you something?

Pride makes you more susceptible to temptation and sin because you have placed yourself in a position of opposition to God. Pride will lead you toward rebellion and disobedience. Pride means that you stop growing because you are not open to instruction. Pride will cause you miss out on the blessings from God.

**The key to receiving grace and more grace is to humble yourself before God and admit your needs.** Then humble yourself before others and allow them to help you. Be open to instruction in your life and receive Godly counsel with joy and thanksgiving. When you stop learning and growing then you have stopped living.

## SOMETHING TO THINK ABOUT:

1. God wants to give you grace and more grace.

2. Are you humble or are you proud?

3. Will you run to the arms of Jesus?

## SOMETHING TO PRAY ABOUT:

Ask God to pour out His grace upon you. Ask Him to reveal if you have pride in your life. If you do then tell Jesus you are sorry and turn from it.

## USE THIS SPACE TO JOURNAL ABOUT WHAT GOD IS SAYING TO YOU:

# DAY SIXTY-NINE – JAMES 4:7

## SOMETHING TO STUDY:

*"Submit yourselves, then, to God. Resist the devil, and he will flee from you."*
James 4:7

We are in the middle of a battle zone. We have an enemy and it's not our parents, our teachers or authority. One of the devil's goals is to see you defeated. Allow me to remind you of 1 Peter 5:8, *"Be self-controlled and alert. Your enemy the devil prowls around like a roaring lion looking for someone to devour."*

The enemy knows our weaknesses and targets them through temptations. How will you respond to the attacks of the enemy? We need to take five specific steps that we are going to look at over the next four days.

- Step one is submit to God. This means you are going to put yourself under His leadership and choose to be obedient to what He is calling you to do. You will call upon the Holy Spirit to fill and control you. You'll confess with your lips what is true and live out that truth day by day, no matter how you feel. You will stop listening to, following and giving into your feelings. Instead you will know the truth and live by God's truth. Be willing to say, "Lord Jesus, I need you! I will do whatever you want me to do." Then be obedient. All the power of the omnipotent God is available to you. Remember what Philippians 4:13 says, *"I can do everything through him who gives me strength."* Now listen to what Ephesians 3:20 says, *"Now to him who is able to do immeasurably more than all we ask or imagine, according to his power that is at work within us."* God is bigger, stronger, smarter and more powerful than our enemy. When you submit to Him, you have nothing to fear. **You are never safer than when you are resting in the arms of Jesus.**

- Step two is resist the devil. First of all, this says to me that you don't have to give into temptation, you actually have a choice. I can choose to give in or I can choose to resist. You will flee from temptation but you never flee from your enemy. You

189

resist the enemy and he flees from you. Second, I am reminded that God will empower us to do whatever He commands us to do. So if He tells us to resist the devil, then He will give us the power and ability to do what He asks us to do. If you were not able to resist the devil or stand against temptation, then God would never command you to do it.

You resist the enemy by putting on the full armor of God. I want you to read about it right now in Ephesians 6:10-18. After reading this I want you to pray out loud, because Satan can't read your mind, and command him and the forces of evil to leave your presence.

What is the result of submitting to God and resisting the devil? He will flee from you and that means temptation will flee with him. Will the temptation ever come back? Yes it will because we are in a battle. Continue to fight by taking these two steps over and over again.

## SOMETHING TO THINK ABOUT:

1. To put on part of the armor of God is not good enough.

2. Are you submitted to God and willing to do whatever He asks?

3. What have you done in the past when you have been tempted?

## SOMETHING TO PRAY ABOUT:

Submit yourself to God and ask Him to fill and control you. Put on the full armor of God and command the forces of evil to be silent and leave your presence in Jesus' name.

## USE THIS SPACE TO JOURNAL ABOUT WHAT GOD IS SAYING TO YOU:

# DAY SEVENTY – JAMES 4:8

## SOMETHING TO STUDY:

*"Come near to God and he will come near to you. Wash your hands, you sinners, and purify your hearts, you double-minded."*
James 4:8

When you are under attack from the enemy and temptation is bearing down on you, God has given you five specific steps that you are to take. Step one is submit yourself to God and step two is resist the devil. Now let's look at the next step.

- Step three is come near to God. If you draw near to God, then He promises to draw near to you. What do you do to prepare yourself to be in God's presence? You need to wash your hands, purify your heart and don't be double-minded.

Your hands represent your actions and lifestyle. To wash your hands means to turn from sin and get right with God. If your hands are dirty, you wash them before shaking someone's hand out of respect for them. Sin dirties your soul. Before coming into God's presence, you need to make yourself presentable by washing through confessing your sins and turning from them.

Next, purify your heart. Why is this important? Out of the overflow of your heart you speak and act. The evil man has an evil heart so evil comes out of his life; the good man has a good heart so goodness comes out of his life. How do you purify your heart? Watch what you put into your mind. **Whatever you take into your mind goes down into your heart.** So if you want a pure heart put pure things into your mind. Study the Word of God and spend time in prayer every day. When you don't feel like reading the Word, do it anyway. When you don't have time to read the Word, make the time. What is more important than spending time with God: getting an education, working, spending time with friends, sports, music, family? All this is important, but not more important than the time you spend with God!

Also, don't be double-minded. When you have dirty hands and an impure heart, you are double-minded because you are trying to live two lives-one for Jesus and the other for the world. However, this doesn't work because bad company corrupts good character. Pretty soon you

191

find your relationship with the Lord becoming distant because you have become a sinner. Your hands and your heart are dirty and you are guilty of sinning against God. Sitting on the fence is choosing the world. Jesus wants to be the Lord of your life. He is not interested in having just a part of you, He wants all of you!

Now you are free to draw near to God and experience Him drawing near to you. Experiencing His personal presence in your life is awesome! Nothing is sweeter than having Jesus Christ, your Savior, Lord and King, near you. Having Him near is to have Him hold you, empower you and deliver you from temptation. This can happen right now as you draw near to Him. The nearer you are to Him the more you will be like Him.

## SOMETHING TO THINK ABOUT:

1. Do you have clean hands and a pure heart?

2. Are you trying to live a double-minded life?

3. Draw near to God and He will draw near to you. What are you going to do?

## SOMETHING TO PRAY ABOUT:

Tell God that you want to be near to Him. Confess your sin and make right your relationship with Him. Thank Him for what He has been doing in and through you.

## USE THIS SPACE TO JOURNAL ABOUT WHAT GOD IS SAYING TO YOU:

# DAY SEVENTY-ONE – JAMES 4:9

## SOMETHING TO STUDY:

*"Grieve, mourn and wail. Change your laughter to mourning and your joy to gloom."*
James 4:9

- Step four is grieve, mourn and wail. That doesn't sound real fun, does it? But remember we aren't talking about learning to dance; we are talking about dealing with temptation in our lives.

When temptation hits, you need to be deeply concerned. Now is not the time for laughter, jokes and complacency. Temptation holds the possibility of sin and that ought to sober you real fast. To sin is to grieve the Holy Spirit, break God's heart and move away from Him. Just the possibility of doing that ought to cause you to grieve, mourn and wail. It is better for your heart to break than to break God's heart.

In the face of temptation, it is time to get serious about the next steps you take. This is a time of preparation for battle. What you do in the next few minutes will either give the enemy a victory or bring glory to God. So change our laughter to mourning and our joy to gloom so that you aren't taking this matter lightly.

You should also be broken for your brothers and sisters who have gone before you and fallen into the same temptation that you are now facing. Grieve for their mistake, mourn for the consequences they are now suffering and wail for God's reputation that has been smeared.

Have you ever gone forward at a camp, retreat or church service and found yourself completely broken before the Lord? What happens? You begin to weep because you see how wrong and sinful you have been. Your heart breaks because you have dishonored the Lord. How do you feel afterwards? Other than exhausted, you feel so good on the inside. **Before we can know real joy, we must be broken before our King.**

Sin or even the potential of sin needs to cause us to weep and mourn.

You should feel badly when you let down a friend, teacher, coach, teammate or parent. But you should feel worse when you let down the Lord. I have seen athletes weep because they missed a last second shot in basketball, struck out in baseball or missed a field goal in football. They aren't just feeling bad for themselves; they feel the weight of letting down their team.

Feeling the weight of sinning and letting down our God reminds us to not make little of the possibilities of sin. Instead, grieve the temptations you face so you don't fall and let Jesus Christ down. Temptation is serious because your spiritual heath and God's reputation are hanging in the balance. Weep now so you can rejoice later.

## SOMETHING TO THINK ABOUT:

1. When is the last time you wept over your sin?

2. To be broken before the Lord is a good thing.

3. Your sin killed Jesus because He chose to die for that sin.

## SOMETHING TO PRAY ABOUT:

Ask God to break your heart over the sin in your life. Tell Him how sorry you are for the bad choices you have made. Remember that Jesus died for the sin you are committing. Pray that you will understand what that means.

## USE THIS SPACE TO JOURNAL ABOUT WHAT GOD IS SAYING TO YOU:

# DAY SEVENTY-TWO – JAMES 4:10

## SOMETHING TO STUDY:

*"Humble yourselves before the Lord, and he will lift you up."*
James 4:10

We have been talking about the steps to take when you are being tempted. Let's review so you remember what you need to do when temptation comes knocking at your door.

- Submit yourself to God.
- Resist the devil.
- Come near to God.
- Grieve, mourn and wail.

And now, can I have a drum roll please, the final step...

- Step five is humble yourself before the Lord. Acknowledge how much you need God - His wisdom, strength and direction. Admit your needs and failures. Don't try to hide things from the Lord. How stupid is that anyway? He sees, knows and hears it all so just be open and honest with Him. Know that you can't overcome temptation by yourself and that you need the Lord and others within the body of Christ to help you.

Humbling yourself is about more than just outward appearance. You and I both know people who look good on the outside, but their hearts are far from God. It's really about being humble on the inside where God can see. It means that you admit your needs and then apply the Word of God to your life and live it out day by day.

Check out Luke 14:11, *"For everyone who exalts himself will be humbled, and he who humbles himself will be exalted."* Why is it so hard to humble yourself? Maybe you think it is a weakness or you are concerned about what other people will think of you. **The truth is that only the strong can humble themselves**. A weak person could never admit their need for God or for anyone. Rather than being concerned about what other people think of you, you should be most concerned about God's opinion of you.

If you will humble yourself, God promises that He will lift you up. He will lift you above the temptation, and will give you wisdom to submit to God. He will give you power to resist the devil, the courage to come near to God, and give you compassion to grieve, mourn and wail. He will give you strength to humble yourself, will lift you up before man and give you favor. You don't have to work, sweat and strive, just trust and obey.

Now that you know the five steps for dealing with temptation, all you need to do is apply them to your life. This is God's word written to teach, rebuke, correct and train you. He gives you these steps so that you can be thoroughly equipped for every good work (2 Timothy 3:16-17).

## SOMETHING TO THINK ABOUT:

1. You can look humble on the outside and still be far from the Lord.

2. Do you need God? Have you told Him that lately?

3. Not allowing others to help you is to be a weak person.

## SOMETHING TO PRAY ABOUT:

Let God know that you need Him. Ask the Lord to lift you up as you humble yourself before Him.

## USE THIS SPACE TO JOURNAL ABOUT WHAT GOD IS SAYING TO YOU:

# DAY SEVENTY-THREE – JAMES 4:11

## SOMETHING TO STUDY:

*"Brothers, do not slander one another. Anyone who speaks against his brother or judges him speaks against the law and judges it. When you judge the law, you are not keeping it, but sitting in judgment on it."*
James 4:11

There is a huge problem in the church today and I bet you see this in your youth group too. What is the problem? The problem is people who slander one another, attack one another verbally and put others down.

To slander is to make someone look bad in another person's eyes. Slandering usually involves making someone look worse than they really are by exaggerating and adding things to your stories. Do you know anyone who gossips and tears other Christians down? Do you ever gossip about your brothers and sisters in Christ? Maybe you just listen to slander. Do you think that is better than doing the slandering yourself? Well, it isn't because you are encouraging that person to be a gossip. You are helping them to sin. When you listen to a gossip, you are just hearing one side of a story, an incomplete story at best, and probably a story filled with lies. Keep this in mind, what a person says to you is some of the stuff they will say about you to others.

When you are with a person who starts to gossip, pick one of these four options:

- Change the subject by asking them questions about themselves. Everyone's favorite subject is themselves!
- Say positive stuff about the person they are slamming. For every negative thing they say, you say a positive. Pretty soon they will get the hint.
- Be direct and say, "Please stop gossiping."
- If the first three don't work, say, "I've got to go." And walk away.

To respond in another way is to sin. **Slander is a cancer that will destroy relationships, friendships and youth ministries.** Satan loves gossip and will do everything he can to encourage you to spread tales about others. We are all guilty of doing some gossiping, but some of us have a major problem with our tongues and we need to face the fact that this is an area of weakness and sin.

The good news is that you can be different. Starting right now you do not have to slander others. Jesus Christ will give you the power to be different. Do not talk about someone, talk to someone. If you have a problem with someone, talk to that person.

Keep in mind that when you are slandering others you are speaking against a son or daughter of God. Would you slander Jesus Christ? Jesus Christ is the Son of God. Isn't the person that you are gossiping about also a son or daughter of God? How absurd would it be to gossip about Jesus? Well, isn't it just as absurd to gossip against your brother or sister in Christ?

On top of everything else, this verse says that when you are judging others you are not keeping the law yourself. Get your Bible and read Matthew 7:3-5. It is saying, in so many words, "You are an idiot!" You are judging someone for the speck in his or her eye, while at the same time you have a plank in your own eye. In other words, take care of your own stuff before you start judging anyone else. Don't you have enough to work on without picking on someone else?

## SOMETHING TO THINK ABOUT:

1. If you are a gossip, stop doing it right now!

2. If you don't listen to a gossip, they won't be gossiping.

3. When was the last time you asked someone to stop slandering?

## SOMETHING TO PRAY ABOUT:

Tell God you are sorry for any slandering that you have done. Ask Him for the power and courage to stop gossiping and to stand against slander.

## USE THIS SPACE TO JOURNAL ABOUT WHAT GOD IS SAYING TO YOU:

# DAY SEVENTY-FOUR – JAMES 4:12

## SOMETHING TO STUDY:

*"There is only one Lawgiver and Judge, the one who is able to save and destroy. But you—who are you to judge your neighbor?"*
James 4:12

Who is the Lawgiver and Judge? If you miss this one you are in big trouble! The answer is God Almighty. He alone is the only one who has the power and the right to save and destroy. When you gossip and slander you are destroying a person, their character, their ministry and their future. Can you save anyone for eternity? No, so stop trying to destroy them.

There are some churches and denominations that spend a lot of time criticizing and slandering other Christians. Is this right or wrong? It is totally and completely wrong. Many of these people come out of what is called "legalistic" churches, denominations and schools. What are these Christians thinking? Do they think this behavior honors the Lord? Do they think they are building up the Body of Christ? Don't these people have anything else they can preach about?

Let me give you some good reasons why you should stop slandering your brothers and sisters in Christ.

- God tells you not to do it. That is the best reason of all.

- Being a judge has some serious consequences. Matthew 7:1-2 says, *"Do not judge, or you too will be judged. For in the same way you judge others, you will be judged, and with the measure you use, it will be measured to you."* If you choose to judge, you will be judged.

- You could not possibly know all the facts about what has happened. You have an incomplete picture of what is actually going on. How can you possibly be a judge of that person?

- We all fall short and sin. We all need Jesus Christ and His mercy and forgiveness. When you judge, you forget that you are a sinner saved by grace. Seeing ourselves correctly will

199

make us more compassionate toward those who have fallen and sinned.

- **There is only one Judge and that is God—it isn't you!**

- When you judge, you take away God's authority. You are saying that you are worthy and have the right to judge others. So, you are claiming the right to be God in their life. How arrogant and wrong is that thinking?

Stop being so critical and negative, stop speaking against your brothers and sisters in Christ and stop being a judge. Who are you to judge your neighbor? You are nobody and the only reason that you are doing anything productive or right is because of what Jesus Christ is doing in and through you. You have no reason to boast or judge.

## SOMETHING TO THINK ABOUT:

1. If you are a part of a church that criticizes and judges, find another church.

2. The fruit of the Spirit doesn't include being judgmental and critical.

3. Treat other people the way you want to be treated.

## SOMETHING TO PRAY ABOUT:

Ask God to give you a heart of compassion for those who are making bad choices and falling into sin. Ask Him to put a guard on your lips so that you do not judge.

## USE THIS SPACE TO JOURNAL ABOUT WHAT GOD IS SAYING TO YOU:

# DAY SEVENTY-FIVE – JAMES 4:13

## SOMETHING TO STUDY:

*"Now listen, you who say, 'Today or tomorrow we will go to this or that city, spend a year there, carry on business and make money'."*
James 4:13

What is wrong with someone planning his or her future? I meet teens all the time who can tell me where they are going to go to college, what they will major in and what kind of job they will have. The problem occurs when we have not consulted God.

There is nothing wrong with planning for the future. As a matter of fact, this is a good thing to do, but you don't want to get ahead of the Lord. The person in this verse is being self-sufficient and planning without God. When you try to take the lead and determine what is best, you are in big trouble. Striking out on your own to do what you want to do is like being a blind man wandering in a jungle, always falling and getting into trouble. **Remember, He is the leader and you are the follower.** It really comes down to the attitude of your heart—a desire on your part to do what the Lord wants you to do.

I live in lovely Rockford, Illinois. It's a very tropical location that sits on the equator and is pretty much seventy degrees all year long. OK, just kidding, it is freezing in the winter and very hot in the summer with a lot of humidity. But now I am off the subject. Chicago is about a ninety-minute drive from Rockford. What if I took you to Chicago, blindfolded you, and told you to walk to Rockford without any help from anyone. You would not make it!

You are doing the very same thing when you plan your life without God. Who knows what is best for you? The correct answer is God, so why would you want to plan your future apart from Him?

How do you include God in your future? Ask Him what He wants you to do. Be willing to go where He wants you to go and do what He wants you to do. My son, Justin, thought he would be going to dental school right out of college, but instead he ended up serving the Lord in Seoul, South Korea. This was not a part of his original plan, but he was willing to go where God wanted Him to go.

I met a girl at a coffee shop who claimed to be a Christian and told me that she decided to go work for a pharmaceutical company. She talked to me about the great pay, retirement, free car, wonderful medical, etc. She had just taken a test and needed to get 90% to pass. This was her second and last time to take the test but she scored 86% so now she may not have a job. She had decided her future apart from God.

When it comes to your future, you can trust your abilities, education, intelligence and training, technology, science, the economy, trends and predictions about the future or you can trust God. The choice is up to you and only you can decide who or what is going to direct your life.

## SOMETHING TO THINK ABOUT:

1. What are your plans for the future?

2. Have you asked God what He wants you to do?

3. Who is best qualified to lead your life?

## SOMETHING TO PRAY ABOUT:

Ask God to lead and direct you. Tell Him that you are happy to put your life in His hands. Let Him know that you trust Him and that you want what He wants for you.

## USE THIS SPACE TO JOURNAL ABOUT WHAT GOD IS SAYING TO YOU:

# DAY SEVENTY-SIX – JAMES 4:14

## SOMETHING TO STUDY:

*"Why, you do not even know what will happen tomorrow. What is your life? You are a mist that appears for a little while and then vanishes."*
James 4:14

Why don't you just plan your own life and do your own thing? Because you don't even know what will happen tomorrow. How many times will you laugh, cry, get hurt, and face crisis? How many times will good things happen? You don't know! You don't have a clue about tomorrow. You say, "I know that I am going to school tomorrow." Really, have you ever been sick and missed school? Not only are you blind to tomorrow, you don't even know what is going to happen in the next hour.

Life is uncertain and you cannot know the future. If you are a Christian that doesn't need to bother you at all because you know that your final destination is heaven. Everything in between is just details. But don't become self-sufficient or cocky about tomorrow. In a split second a car accident or medical exam can totally alter your future. All your priorities, hopes and dreams can be radically changed.

Still, we strut around like we have it all under control and know exactly what is going to happen in our lives. Wake up and realize that you are a moment away from disaster! Get an attitude check; you have no reason to be arrogant or proud. Nothing you do in your own power lasts or impresses the Lord. Do you think that God is impressed because you have earned 100 million dollars? Does athletic ability impress Him? How impressed have you been this week with the ants in your backyard? Ants can lift 20 times their own body weight; that would be like a second grader being able to lift a car! Pretty impressive, but chances are you don't really care. We aren't impressed, awed, intimidated or fearful of ants. In the same way, God is not impressed with our own abilities.

What is our life? It is a mist that appears for a little while and then vanishes. A mist is not permanent. You see it for a short time and then it disappears. Few people will remember you or care about your life. You learn about famous people in history class, but do you really care? Many of us are bored and only remember names to pass a test.

What can you count on for sure? One day you will die, unless Jesus returns, and you can depend on God Almighty.

Few of us will know when our death is coming or how it will occur. But we do know that it is coming and then we will step into eternity. How impressed will God be with an all-star athlete or a movie star when they stand before Him? **All we bring to eternity is our self and what we did for the cause of Christ.**

Who knows what is going to happen to you tomorrow— you or God? With this in mind, does it make more sense to trust yourself or to trust God with your life?

## SOMETHING TO THINK ABOUT:

1. What are you planning to do with your life?

2. Who are you trying to impress with your life?

3. What are you totally sure about?

## SOMETHING TO PRAY ABOUT:

Tell God that you trust Him with your life and your tomorrows. Thank Him for your life. Now think of at least twenty-five things that you can thank God for and spend the rest of the time in praise and thanksgiving.

## USE THIS SPACE TO JOURNAL ABOUT WHAT GOD IS SAYING TO YOU:

# DAY SEVENTY-SEVEN – JAMES 4:15

## SOMETHING TO STUDY:

"Instead, you ought to say, 'If it is the Lord's will, we will live and do this or that'."
James 4:15

It all goes back to the question, "Why do you exist?" You exist to glorify Jesus Christ and make Him look good by what you say and do. You acknowledge that He is King of Kings and Lord of your life. You say, "God, here is my life and if it is your will I will go here and do this or that." You are confessing your dependence on God and your willingness to follow Him wherever He leads.

As a senior in high school, I decided that I would be an oceanographer and study the great white shark. I would go to a University in California and eventually transfer to Scripts Institute of Oceanography. During my senior year, I met Jesus Christ and He radically changed my life. I ended up going to Bethel University in St. Paul, Minnesota. While at Bethel, I decided that I would be an elementary school teacher. Right before I graduated, I received a call from Sunny Ridge Home in Wheaton, Illinois. They offered me the job of men's caseworker for delinquent and emotionally disturbed teenagers. While at Sunny Ridge, God developed in me a love for teenagers and a passion to work with them. If I hadn't listened to the Lord, I would be shark bait right now and I wouldn't be fulfilled because I would not be doing what God created me to do.

God knows you better than you know yourself. He knows your gifts, talents and abilities. He has a purpose, plan and destiny for your life. It is fine for you to dream dreams and make plans for the future. Just make sure that you are asking God for His input and direction and be willing to go where He leads you even if it isn't what you had planned. In other words, say, "If it is your will I will live here and do this." **Be open to God's leading in your life.**

You can choose to do whatever you want to do. You can head in the opposite direction of where God wants you to be and turn your back on His will for your life. The Lord always gives you the awesome privilege of choice. But you will never be happier than when you are in the very center of God's will, doing what He wants you to do.

I can't imagine doing anything else, I love my job and I love being able to speak and invest my life in the lives of teenagers. I am where I am today not because of my intellect or hard work, but because I listened to the still small voice of God, desired to do His will and was obedient. God can and will take good care of you if you'll follow Him.

Proverbs 3:6 says, *"In all your ways acknowledge him, and he will make your paths straight."*

## SOMETHING TO THINK ABOUT:

1. Are you seeking to fulfill your will or God's will?

2. Are you asking God what He wants you to do and are you willing to obey?

3. If you are making a poor choice now, what makes you think you will make the right choice about your future?

## SOMETHING TO PRAY ABOUT:

Tell God what you would like to do with your future, but tell Him, "I only want it if this is what you will for me."

## USE THIS SPACE TO JOURNAL ABOUT WHAT GOD IS SAYING TO YOU:

# DAY SEVENTY-EIGHT – JAMES 4:16

## SOMETHING TO STUDY:

*"As it is, you boast and brag. All such boasting is evil."*
James 4:16

Pride and self-sufficiency lead to boasting and bragging. When you say, "I will do this and go here and this is what I am doing with my life," you are not taking into consideration God's will. What if your plan for your life isn't God's plan for your life? Who is in control? Are you making all the decisions or do you allow the Lord to lead and direct you?

I get real tired, real fast with people who brag and boast about themselves. My son, Garrett, came back from a winter retreat where the speaker spent a lot of time talking about how great he is and all the things he has done and how you should buy his book. Teenagers can see right through this and it is a major turn off. **It is better to allow others to say nice things about you.**

Sometimes you boast with your life. You don't have to say anything, but you like to show everyone all of your stuff: designer clothes, hot car (or in my case hot family van), sound system, computer, big screen TV and Batman PJs. Or maybe you show off your abilities: skating, surfing, team sports, karate, judo, chop suey, dance, music, drama and other things at which you excel. All this is a form of bragging and boasting, showing other people why you are so great and wonderful.

When you boast and brag, it means that you are falling into the comparison trap. Comparing leads to judging and being critical. I am better than you because of what I have or what I do. You spend your whole life feeling superior or inferior. That is crazy! You are not to compare yourself to anyone— you are neither superior nor inferior. You are just yourself and that is something good to be.

Sometimes you boast to cover up your weaknesses. You feel inadequate so you try to make yourself look better or make others look worse. Boasting is evil because it seeks to glorify you and leads to comparing, judging and being critical. The enemy uses bragging and boasting to center your attention on yourself rather than on God.

It is not wrong to want attention; it is all tied into our need to be loved. However, how you gain that attention can be very wrong. If you have to be the center of attention and you brag on yourself while looking down on others that is wrong. Be happy with who you are because God made you. Instead of bragging and boasting, seek to build others up and be most excited about your relationship with Jesus Christ. As you honor God, He will honor you and give you favor in other people's eyes.

It is much better to let God honor you rather than trying to honor yourself. Humility will build respect while bragging will lead to disgust from others.

## SOMETHING TO THINK ABOUT:

1. Do you boast and brag with your words or your life?

2. Are you comparing yourself to others?

3. All you have and all you are come from God.

## SOMETHING TO PRAY ABOUT:

Thank God for all the abilities and blessing that He has poured out on your life. Ask Him to convict you of any bragging and boasting that you are doing.

## USE THIS SPACE TO JOURNAL ABOUT WHAT GOD IS SAYING TO YOU:

# DAY SEVENTY-NINE – JAMES 4:17

## SOMETHING TO STUDY:

*"Anyone, then, who knows the good he ought to do and doesn't do it, sins."*
James 4:17

We talk a lot about what we need to stop doing: drinking, smoking, drugs, being sexually active and kicking small furry animals. When we disobey God and do what He tells us not to do, we understand that we are sinning.

Now God is taking it a step further. If you know that there is something good that God is calling you to do and you don't do it, you are sinning. What are some things that God has been calling you to do?

- Reach out to a visitor in youth group.
- Tell someone about Jesus.
- Love the unlovely.
- Show your teachers respect.
- Obey your parents.
- Buy a homeless person a meal.
- Eat lunch with someone who is sitting alone.

Refusing to do what God tells you to do is sin. Are you willing to fulfill God's will for your life? The Lord does have a purpose, plan and destiny for your life, but what good is it if you aren't willing to follow? The more you are obedient to God the more He will lead and direct you.

Remember, evil triumphs when good does nothing. You combat evil with good when you choose to do what God is calling you to do. You have all of God's power available when you step out in obedience to do the good He is calling you to do.

When you do good you are following God's will for your life. Refusing to do good is only hurting you in the long run. Matthew 7:26-27 says, *"But everyone who hears these words of mine and does not put them into practice is like a foolish man who built his house on sand. The rain came down, the streams rose, and the winds blew and beat against that house, and it fell with a great crash."*

209

The choices you are making now are laying a foundation for your life. Doing what God is calling you to do sets a firm foundation. Refusing to do what God is calling you to do is like building a house on sand. We all have seen what storms do to houses that are built on or near the sand.

**What you are doing today is what you are becoming tomorrow.** If you are going to follow the Lord and do His will in the future, start now by doing what is good today.

## SOMETHING TO THINK ABOUT:

1. What are some good things that the Lord wants you to do?

2. God has a plan for your life. Are you willing to follow that plan?

3. I am most fulfilled when I am doing what God has called me to do.

## SOMETHING TO PRAY ABOUT:

Ask God what He wants you to do and tell Him that you will be obedient to Him. Tell Him that you are sorry for the times when He has asked you to do something good and you didn't do it.

## USE THIS SPACE TO JOURNAL ABOUT WHAT GOD IS SAYING TO YOU:

# DAY EIGHTY – JAMES 5:1

## SOMETHING TO STUDY:

*"Now listen, you rich people, weep and wail because of the*
*misery that is coming upon you."*
James 5:1

God is not against rich people, but the next several devotions
are a warning against people who have money and hoard it for
themselves rather than use it to help others. Where does your money
come from? It comes from the Lord who has given you the mind,
strength and favor to do the job for which you are paid. Some people
have incredible wealth and with that privilege comes the responsibility
to spend and invest that money wisely—to share with others and put
the money to use in a way that will glorify Jesus Christ.

If you hoard your money and only spend it on yourself, God
says to weep and wail because misery is coming upon you. What is that
misery?

- You become a selfish person.
- Money becomes your God.
- The hours that you work, to earn the money that you think will
  make you happy, will kill you emotionally and physically and
  destroy relationships.
- You will experience emptiness and loneliness.
- Ultimately you will be weeping in hell if you don't know Jesus.

Money is a terrible substitute for the will of God. **Don't settle for
money when God desires so much more for you.** Money will not
bring you joy, peace or fulfillment. These things come from God.

Is it wrong to have money? No, but that is not what is most
important. Take the money that God has blessed you with and use it to
help those around you. Be generous and gracious with God's money.
The great news is that you can't out give God and the more you give
the more He will bless your life.

You need to have your priorities set and keep the main thing the
main thing. I led teens on short-term mission trips for many years and I
would be a rich man if I had a dollar for every time some student said

211

to me, "I can't go because I need to make money." You don't need to make money; you need to serve God! If He is calling you to make money, then do it. But I want to suggest that most of us don't even ask God if He wants us to work. We just assume that the right thing to do is getting a job and making some money. What are you making money for: car, college, clothes, stuff, etc.? That is not bad in and of itself, but it is bad if God wanted you to do something else.

Be warned that if your priorities are messed up, if money is most important to you and if you are selfish with money, you should be prepared for weeping and wailing because misery is about to hit you.

## SOMETHING TO THINK ABOUT:

1. How important is money to you?

2. Are you generous with your money? Can God trust you with money?

3. You don't need a job—you need Jesus!

## SOMETHING TO PRAY ABOUT:

Ask God what He wants you to do with your money. Tell Him that you will be generous with the money that He has given you.

## USE THIS SPACE TO JOURNAL ABOUT WHAT GOD IS SAYING TO YOU:

# DAY EIGHTY-ONE – JAMES 5:2

## SOMETHING TO STUDY:

*"Your wealth has rotted, and moths have eaten your clothes."*
James 5:2

**When it comes to your life, what is really going to last?** You are leaving a legacy to future generations. What will happen to all your money? It will rot, decay and pass away. Hey, that rhymed and you could probably make a song out of it! Now back to the devotion. What will happen to all those stylish clothes that you had to have to impress people you didn't really even like? They will fall apart and go out of style. The moth will eat it and it will be no more. What will happen to that car you so desperately wanted? It will be scrapes, scratches, dents and worse. It will break down and fall apart.

Use your money in a way that will build the kingdom of God and make the Lord look good...

- First of all, take a portion of your money to your local church (ten percent of what you are making) and put it in the offering plate. Bonnie and I do that first; before we pay any bills or do anything else with our money, we first give to the Lord.

- Second, look for a missionary who you could support personally. Write them a letter and send them some money. Who should you support? Look for someone who is ministering in a country that you have a heart for or who is involved in a ministry that you think is really important.

- Third, how about adopting a child overseas that you could support and help? It will probably cost you just over one dollar a day and that money will be used to help feed, cloth and educate the child.

- Fourth, how about supporting some local ministries like a crisis pregnancy center, homeless shelter, home for abused women and children, or soup kitchen?

Maybe you can't support all four of these areas, but do something. Be sure that you support your local church and after that ask God where

He wants you to invest your money. I want you to be able to go to movies, eat out, buy some games and do stuff with your friends, but if that is all you are spending your money on then you are missing out on what God is calling you to do. God wants you to learn to be sacrificial and lay down your life for the cause of Christ. He desires that you freely give of yourself and your resources and give back to Him what He has already given to you.

Right now you are developing patterns that will carry you for the rest of your life. How do you want to be remembered— as someone who held onto their money and accumulated stuff or someone who used their money to impact the world for the kingdom of God? Spend your money wisely now so that you will spend your money wisely in the future.

## SOMETHING TO THINK ABOUT:

1. What do you spend your money on?

2. Who do you support financially?

3. How do you want to be remembered, as selfish or sacrificial?

## SOMETHING TO PRAY ABOUT:

Ask God to show you where you can give your money that will help others. Ask Him to lay organizations and individuals on your heart that you can help.

## USE THIS SPACE TO JOURNAL ABOUT WHAT GOD IS SAYING TO YOU:

# DAY EIGHTY-TWO – JAMES 5:3

## SOMETHING TO STUDY:

*"Your gold and silver are corroded. Their corrosion will testify against you and eat your flesh like fire. You have hoarded wealth in the last days."*
James 5:3

Your wealth will pass away; it will never bring you lasting happiness. God has not blessed you financially so that you can keep the money for yourself. He wants you to give it away and help others. Do you ever save money for yourself? Yes, we need to live and put away for the future, but be generous with your money. One day your wealth will be taken away from you and you will be held accountable for what you did with the money the Lord gave you. Money is not bad, but how your heart responds to money can be very bad. 1 Timothy 6:9-10 says, *"People who want to get rich fall into temptation and a trap and into many foolish and harmful desires that plunge men into ruin and destruction. For the love of money is a root of all kinds of evil. Some people, eager for money, have wandered from the faith and pierced themselves with many griefs."*

Money can eat your flesh like fire and pierce you with many griefs. You lust for money and the more you get the more you want and it never satisfies. It will begin to consume you and destroy you on the inside like fire can eat your flesh. Everything else takes a backseat to money. Friends, family and God lose importance in your life because you think that money is going to make you happy. It will lead you into temptation, compromise, spiritual failure, foolish and harmful desires, ruin, destruction and heartache. How many of you have heard this, "Study hard so that you can get a good job and make a lot of money so you can live a comfortable life?" **Your priority is not to make a lot of money, God never called you to a comfortable life.** He has called you to step out in faith and do what He is calling you to do. Money can become like a poison that slowly kills you spiritually and emotionally.

What good does it do to hoard wealth in the last days? It becomes worthless and useless as it is all taken from you. A wealthy man died and someone asked, "How much money did he leave?" The answer was, "All of it." You aren't going to take it with you. Use it now to glorify God and help others.

It is a mistake to think there is security in wealth. In 1929 there was the stock market crash. Men had gone to bed safe, content and very wealthy, but woke up the next morning to find that all their money was gone. What did they do? Many committed suicide. Do not allow money to come between you and your God or to become your God.

Psalm 62:10b, *"...though your riches increase, do not set your heart on them."*

Proverbs 22:1-2, *"A good name is more desirable than great riches; to be esteemed is better than silver or gold. Rich and poor have this in common: The Lord is the Maker of them all."*

## SOMETHING TO THINK ABOUT:

1. Do you put your hope in God or money?

2. A good name and being esteemed is better than money. Do you believe that?

3. Whose money is it—yours or God's?

## SOMETHING TO PRAY ABOUT:

Ask God what he wants you to do with His money. Tell Him that you desire a good name and esteem more than riches.

## USE THIS SPACE TO JOURNAL ABOUT WHAT GOD IS SAYING TO YOU:

# DAY EIGHTY-THREE – JAMES 5:4

## SOMETHING TO STUDY:

*"Look! The wages you failed to pay the workmen who mowed your fields are crying out against you. The cries of the harvesters have reached the ears of the Lord Almighty."*
James 5:4

I realize that not many of you have someone mowing your fields. As a matter of fact, if anyone is doing any mowing it is probably you! But let's look at the broader meaning, which is ripping people off—not giving them what they deserve and earned.

Through the years I have been ripped off and the sad fact is that no one rips you off like another Christian. I have had groups book me to speak and then cancel at the last minute. They refuse to pay me anything, even though this is my main form of income. I have had people take books, CDs and tapes telling me they would send me a check and no check ever comes. One time a church asked me to come and speak on a Sunday. I had to drive about one hour each way. No one volunteered to take us out to eat and they handed me a check for twenty-five dollars. I lost money speaking for them.

What do I do? Do I contact a lawyer and sue them? No, I cry out against them to God and He takes care of me and judges them. I think that most of the groups that have ripped me off think they have gotten away with it, but in reality they are suffering for their actions. I am sure that some have not even connected the two, but things are going poorly for them because they have done what is wrong in God's eyes.

How about you, have you ripped anyone off? Have you ever shoplifted, borrowed money and never paid it back, taken advantage of an employer by not working as hard as you should, held back respect from a teacher, used someone sexually, taken advantage of your parents? What do you need to do?

- Go to the store, confess what you did and volunteer to pay them back.
- Pay back all the money that you borrowed.

- Apologize to the employer and volunteer to work some hours for free.
- Tell the teacher that you are sorry for being rude and start showing them respect.
- Humble yourself and apologize for using them sexually and pursue purity.
- Talk to your parents and share what you have done wrong. Ask them to forgive you and then begin to obey your parents.

Your sin cries out to God and He will judge you. You haven't gotten away with anything. Things will continue to go poorly for you until you do what is right and make restitution to the people you have wronged.

## SOMETHING TO THINK ABOUT:

1. Have you ripped anyone off?

2. What do you need to do to make things right?

3. **Honor the Lord and He will honor you.**

## SOMETHING TO PRAY ABOUT:

Ask God to lay on your heart anyone you have ripped off. Tell Him you will be obedient and ask Him to please remove His judgment from your life as you make right the wrongs you have committed.

## USE THIS SPACE TO JOURNAL ABOUT WHAT GOD IS SAYING TO YOU:

# DAY EIGHTY-FOUR – JAMES 5:5

## SOMETHING TO STUDY:

> *"You have lived on earth in luxury and self-indulgence. You have fattened yourselves in the day of slaughter."*
> James 5:5

Look around you at all the slaughter that is going on due to wars, earthquakes, volcanoes, tsunamis, hurricanes, tornados, disease, starvation, etc. Yet, we sit back in luxury and self-indulgence. We care more about our comfort than the suffering of those around us. We must wake up! As a country and as individuals, we are blessed. With that blessing comes a responsibility to use the money and resources we have to help others.

> Proverbs 3:27, *"Do not withhold good from those who deserve it, when it is in your power to act."*
>
> Luke 8:14, *"The seed that fell among thorns stands for those who hear, but as they go on their way they are choked by life's worries, riches and pleasures, and they do not mature."*
>
> Luke 12:15, *"Then he said to them, 'Watch out! Be on your guard against all kinds of greed; a man's life does not consist in the abundance of his possessions'."*

If we live our whole lives in luxury and self-indulgence, without using our money as God intended, we are setting ourselves up for slaughter. It is like the cow that eats all day and doesn't realize it is being fattened for its eventual slaughter.

To spend all your money on yourself, to seek luxury, to be self-indulgent, to be mainly concerned with your comfort, to not be moved by the suffering of those around you, to ignore the poor and to hoard your money would call into question whether you are really a Christian. If you aren't a Christian, then you are fattening yourself for the ultimate slaughter and that is hell.

*"Then he will say to those on his left, 'Depart from me, you who are cursed, into the eternal fire prepared for the devil and his angels. For I was hungry and you gave me nothing to eat, I was thirsty and you gave*

219

*me nothing to drink, I was a stranger and you did not invite me in, I needed clothes and you did not clothe me, I was sick and in prison and you did not look after me'. They also will answer, 'Lord, when did we see you hungry or thirsty or a stranger or needing clothes or sick or in prison, and did not help you?' He will reply, 'I tell you the truth, whatever you did not do for one of the least of these, you did not do for me.' Then they will go away to eternal punishment, but the righteous to eternal life,"* Matthew 25:41-46

## SOMETHING TO THINK ABOUT:

1. What needs do you see around you?

2. Who needs help that you have the ability to touch?

3. Are you living in luxury and self-indulgence?

## SOMETHING TO PRAY ABOUT:

Ask God to change your attitude toward the poor and needy. Ask Him to motivate you to action. Tell Him you will use your time and resources to help those in need.

## USE THIS SPACE TO JOURNAL ABOUT WHAT GOD IS SAYING TO YOU:

# DAY EIGHTY-FIVE – JAMES 5:6

## SOMETHING TO STUDY:

*"You have condemned and murdered innocent men, who were not opposing you."*
James 5:6

Are you guilty of hurting innocent people? I hope you haven't killed anyone, but how many people have you hurt with your words? How many people have you been rude and cruel towards?

The rich believe they can do almost anything. They think that money means power and that laws don't apply to them. Rich people say, "I get what I want, I do what I want and I don't care who I hurt." Count every time you read the word I in that last sentence. For them, it's all about me, me, me. By the way, I am not talking about rich Christians who truly love Jesus.

Our culture esteems and honors those with money. Even though they may be rude, messed up, drug addicted, divorced, law breaking, living in sin, using other people, or drunks, others are still willing to overlook all of that if the person has money. Today a person can even commit a crime and get away with it if they have a lot of money and can afford the best lawyers.

We value the opinions of the rich and listen to them when they speak on a variety of subjects from politics to marriage. They may not have graduated from high school and may be living in sin, but we listen to them because they are the rich and famous. We just assume they must know what they are talking about, but they don't!

Is this what Jesus values? Was Jesus rich? Does He want us to be most concerned with money and power? No! He is more interested in what is happening inside our lives. Money becomes a mask that people wear so that they don't have to deal with all the other problems in their lives. **The world values money and Jesus values character. The world values power and Jesus values humility.**

Do not buy into the things of this world. I have said it before; money does not make you happy, bring you peace of mind or fulfill you. In some cases, it does just the opposite. One day you wake up and discover that you are miserable, stressed and empty on the inside.

Read today's verse again. It is bad enough to hurt people who are against you, but to hurt someone who is innocent and does not oppose you is just cruel, arrogant and mean. With your words and actions, you are either building up or tearing down. Seek to be known for caring and not cruelty, concern and not gossip, love and not hate. These are choices that you can make each and every day. Today, do not condemn the innocent, do not be a bully.

## SOMETHING TO THINK ABOUT:

1. How are you treating the people around you that are poor in money, talents, abilities, looks, style, etc?

2. Who have you respected more: someone with money and power or someone with character and humility?

3. What do you desire for your future?

## SOMETHING TO PRAY ABOUT:

Ask God to give you a heart for the poor and ask Him to open the door so that you can reach out in love to those the world sees as poor.

## USE THIS SPACE TO JOURNAL ABOUT WHAT GOD IS SAYING TO YOU:

# DAY EIGHTY-SIX – JAMES 5:7

## SOMETHING TO STUDY:

*"Be patient, then, brothers, until the Lord's coming. See how the farmer waits for the land to yield its valuable crop and how patient he is for the autumn and spring rains."*
James 5:7

It does no good to worry or be anxious. You can't rush the rain and you can't rush the land to yield its crops. They will come in time so be patient. You need to be patient until the Lord comes. Life is hard, but heaven will be awesome; people can be a pain, but Jesus is the best; today is frustrating, but eternity will be amazing. Be patient and don't give up, don't give in and don't walk away.

Why do you need to be patient until the Lord's coming? After the Lord returns, you will have everything you ever wanted, needed or dreamed of. You won't have to be patient because you won't be lacking anything. Today may be hard, frustrating and a big fat hassle, but be patient. Be patient because God is coming back. Be patient because He is near. Be patient because He is teaching you. Be patient because He is sovereign and has it all under control.

Everything pales in comparison to the Lord's coming. Will you be ready for that great day? Don't worry about how you look, don't worry about what you will eat, what you will wear, about grades, people and stuff. But, be very worried if you don't know Jesus and aren't prepared for His return. If you do know Him, everything else pales in comparison to that fact. You can be patient and at peace with yourself, others and God because your eternity is set.

**Patience doesn't mean that you sit around and do nothing.** You are patient like the farmer. Do you think that the farmer works hard? Yes, he works from morning to evening doing what needs to be done. What good does it do him to patiently wait for the crops if he hasn't sowed the seeds first? We do what God is calling us to do and we work hard. We desire to become everything the Lord has created us to be. We do what we can, through the power of the Holy Spirit, and leave the rest in God's hands.

Patience is not one of my strong points. I want things and I want them now. I am always in a hurry and that leads to frustration and anger on my part. I need to learn to wait patiently for God and in the meantime do what is right. How about you?

## SOMETHING TO THINK ABOUT:

1. Are you prepared for the Lord to return?

2. How patient have you been today, last week, this month?

3. What do you need to place in God's hands and stop worrying about?

## SOMETHING TO PRAY ABOUT:

Ask God if you are prepared to meet Him when He returns. Ask Him if there are any things you need to stop or start doing to prepare for that day. Ask Him to develop patience in your life.

## USE THIS SPACE TO JOURNAL ABOUT WHAT GOD IS SAYING TO YOU:

# DAY EIGHTY-SEVEN – JAMES 5:8

## SOMETHING TO STUDY:

*"You too, be patient and stand firm, because the Lord's coming is near."*
James 5:8

We are so worried and in a hurry about everything. What is weighing you down, causing you to worry, and bringing you down? The pressure for good grades, having to do well on your SAT's, relationships that are driving you crazy, a job that is a lot of work and not a lot of pay, family problems, demanding coaches, and, and, and... I am sure you can add a lot to this list. What is my suggestion for you? Be patient, stand firm and wait on the Lord. This sounds very similar to yesterday's devotions, hmmm, maybe God is trying to tell you something.

God adds something to being patient and that is standing firm—to remain strong in your faith and beliefs, refusing to compromise and living for Jesus each and every day.

*"For the time will come when men will not put up with sound doctrine. Instead, to suit their own desires, they will gather around them a great number of teachers to say what their itching ears want to hear. They will turn their ears away from the truth and turn aside to myths,"* 2 · Timothy 4:3-4. Will this be you or will you stand firm in your faith?

We see people turning from the truth today in the church. Some pastors have stopped preaching the truth and have sold out to what is politically correct or popular. Where do you find the truth? You can find truth in the Bible—that is God's truth to us and it does not change. If anyone contradicts the Word of God, they are WRONG. That is why it is so important that you know what the Word says so that you don't allow others to deceive you.

The other day I was watching TV in my hotel room and a popular, young preacher came on so I decided to listen to him. He misused scripture, taught some new age stuff, talked about getting what you want and how you deserve the best. I was appalled and now he has this best-selling book out that is just as bad. It makes me sad to think that thousands of people are listening to this man and believing everything he says without checking out the Bible and calling him on his errors.

We don't really want the truth today because it is hard. I don't want to love the unlovely. I don't want to give the first part of my paycheck to the Lord. I don't want to obey my parents. I don't want to go on the mission field. I don't want to be sexually pure. I don't want to stop gossiping. Instead, I want to do what feels good to me at the moment. So, I find people who will tell me it is OK to do the things that I shouldn't be doing. Instead we need to be willing to give up instant gratification for the much greater satisfaction of living for Jesus now!

The great news is that the Lord's coming is nearer today than it was yesterday. Be patient, don't give up and stand firm in your faith. **God will honor those who honor Him.** Today choose to honor Him by what you say and do!

## SOMETHING TO THINK ABOUT:

1. Are you studying the Word of God? Thanks for using my book, but you need to make sure that you are digging into and studying the Bible.

2. Do you choose to do what is right or what feels good?

3. Are you standing firm in the faith?

## SOMETHING TO PRAY ABOUT:

Ask God to give you wisdom and understanding so that you can see what is true and what is false. Ask Him to give you a love and passion for His Word.

## USE THIS SPACE TO JOURNAL ABOUT WHAT GOD IS SAYING TO YOU:

# DAY EIGHTY-EIGHT – JAMES 5:9

## SOMETHING TO STUDY:

*"Don't grumble against each other, brothers, or you will be judged.
The Judge is standing at the door!"*
James 5:9

Stop grumbling against other Christians. We are so fast to complain because people are not doing what we think they should do. Today we complain and grumble against styles of music, messages we don't like and decisions we don't agree with. We must always confront sin, but when it comes to differences of opinion we must stop judging just because we don't agree.

God is aware of everything you say, think and do (even in the dark where you didn't think anyone could see). How disgusting has your thought life been over the last several months? Do you want God judging you? Then stop judging others just because you don't agree on issues that are not sin issues.

You would be amazed at the things people would grumble at me about when I was a youth pastor. They didn't like the fact that our music was too contemporary. They didn't like that I pulled the teenagers out of Sunday night service to do our own youth worship service. They didn't like that I showed movie or TV clips on Sunday morning. They grumbled because we didn't have enough socials—you name it and they probably grumbled about it. This grumbling sucks the joy and emotional strength out of you. Stop doing that to your youth pastor or senior pastor because God is standing at the door of your heart and He will be your judge.

Get your eyes off of everyone else and focus on Jesus Christ. **If you are more focused on Jesus, you will be less focused on yourself.** The world does not revolve around you and this is not about what you like or want. It is all about you laying down your life and seeking to serve others.

When you grumble, you cause dissention and cliques within the body of Christ. God is not happy when you do this; it doesn't please Him. Do you think He wants His church divided and grumbling against each other? We become a terrible example to the non-Christian. How can we love the non-Christian when we can't even get along as Christians?

Here is a creative idea—pray for the people you disagree with instead of grumbling against them. Remember what mom used to say. "If you don't have anything good to say then don't say anything at all." It might be a good idea if you kept your mouth shut. We all have our own faults, don't we? So be compassionate and merciful toward others!

## SOMETHING TO THINK ABOUT:

1. Have you been grumbling about your brothers or sisters in Christ?

2. Do you want God to judge you?

3. Do you need to apologize for grumbling? If you have grumbled then you need to say you are sorry.

## SOMETHING TO PRAY ABOUT:

Ask God to convict you of any grumbling or criticizing done against other Christians. Ask Him to reveal if there is anyone you need to apologize to for grumbling. Ask God not to judge you and ask Him to give you the grace and wisdom to treat others the way Jesus Christ treats you.

## USE THIS SPACE TO JOURNAL ABOUT WHAT GOD IS SAYING TO YOU:

# DAY EIGHTY-NINE – JAMES 5:10

## SOMETHING TO STUDY:

*"Brothers, as an example of patience in the face of suffering, take the prophets who spoke in the name of the Lord."*
James 5:10

Here James gives us the example of the prophets who suffered for speaking truth about God and for God. They were obedient and sought to live for God. What happened to them? Did they receive a lot of money, big chariots, nice houses and things of the world? No, they ended up suffering. **Remember that God doesn't keep you from suffering, but sustains you in the midst of the suffering.**

Being obedient to the Lord doesn't mean you will be free from suffering and problems. However, through all your problems, God will seek to develop and mold you into His image. Problems are not bad; they are not the real issue. The real issue is how you respond to the problem. God's desire is that you would be patient and wait on Him.

We are under the misconception that if we really love Jesus, we will not suffer. We think that suffering is only a result of sin and disobedience, but that is not true. 2 Timothy 3:12 says, *"In fact, everyone who wants to live a godly life in Christ Jesus will be persecuted..."* If you determine to live for Jesus, you will encounter suffering.

In the midst of your suffering, God cares for you and will help you. He is your rock and your salvation. You can depend on Him to protect and provide for you. He understands like no one else and He has a purpose, plan and destiny for you. When suffering comes, stand firm in the Lord and be patient. He will see you through it and you will be better off and closer to Him because of the suffering you have experienced.

God will use you as an example to others about what it means to faithfully follow after the King of Kings. How small is your faith in Christ when you give up the first time you face suffering? It is easy to follow the Lord when things are going well, but what happens when things get hard? Do you stay faithful or do you turn away? Take a stand for Jesus and you lose popularity, people make fun of you and you suffer. Will God find you patient in your suffering or will you turn back to the things of this world and try to escape the suffering at any cost?

Suffering is never fun, but it is not bad for us. It shows us what is really important and helps us reset our priorities; it draws us to Jesus Christ and keeps us more dependent on Him. 1 Peter 5:10 says, *"And the God of all grace, who called you to his eternal glory in Christ, after you have suffered a little while, will himself restore you and make you strong, firm and steadfast."*

## SOMETHING TO THINK ABOUT:

1. What has God taught you through your suffering?

2. Will you serve the Lord when things get really hard?

3. Be patient in your suffering so that you can learn everything the Lord is trying to teach you.

## SOMETHING TO PRAY ABOUT:

Ask God to open your eyes to everything He is trying to teach you. Tell Him that you will be patient in the midst of suffering. Ask Him for His strength and courage to stand strong.

## USE THIS SPACE TO JOURNAL ABOUT WHAT GOD IS SAYING TO YOU:

# DAY NINETY – JAMES 5:11

## SOMETHING TO STUDY:

*"As you know, we consider blessed those who have persevered. You have heard of Job's perseverance and have seen what the Lord finally brought about. The Lord is full of compassion and mercy."*
James 5:11

Do you know stories of godly men and women who have persevered? Their stories inspire us as we see how much God has loved and blessed those who stand strong in the midst of tremendous trials and suffering.

Few of us will ever suffer as much as Job suffered. He lost everything and yet refused to turn from God. He didn't understand everything that was happening to him, but he never gave up and he trusted God. If you haven't read the story of Job, take your Bible and read it now. It is forty-two chapters long so it will take a little bit of your time. In the first three chapters, you learn about Job's problems. He loses everything except his wife and she encourages him to commit suicide. In chapters four through thirty-seven, we see Job standing up to the accusations and questions of his three friends. By the way, with friends like Job's, you don't really need enemies. Chapters thirty-eight through forty-two have God first humbling Job, then honoring him and giving him twice as much as he had before the suffering happened.

Job could persevere because He believed that God was in control. God will always save us—if not in this life, then in the life to come. When we focus on the fact that one day we will inherit all of eternity, our present suffering doesn't have to overwhelm us.

People used to say that if you're wealthy and comfortable, you must be blessed by God, but if you're poor and suffering, you must be cursed by God. Look around and you will see that people still believe this and it is TOTALLY wrong. Our brothers and sisters in Christ around the world are suffering and poor, yet great is their reward in heaven. On the other hand, there are people here in the US who are very wealthy and comfortable, but they are a heartbeat away from spending eternity in hell.

Suffering is not necessarily a result of sin. **God has a higher purpose for suffering—to teach, develop and mold us into His image.** Our suffering is preparing us for the future and what the Lord is going to do in and through us. It is bringing to the surface the areas that we need to work on and reveals to us what our faith is really like. There is nothing like a little suffering to find out if we really love Jesus and are willing to follow Him.

The great news is that God is full of compassion and mercy. He understands, He will take care of us and show us mercy as we wait on Him. He desires the very best for us and that may include suffering. As a loving parent, I have allowed my child to suffer a little to save them from a much greater pain later on. For example, I had them get immunizations even though the shots hurt. I did this because I knew the diseases they might get later on would cause greater suffering. So God allows us to suffer a little now to save us from a much greater pain later on. Then one day we will gain all of heaven which will make the suffering all worthwhile.

## SOMETHING TO THINK ABOUT:

1. When suffering comes, do you give up or do you follow Jesus?

2. Suffering reveals what our faith is really like.

3. God's grace is sufficient for you.

## SOMETHING TO PRAY ABOUT:

Tell God you want to learn during suffering and that you will wait for Him.

## USE THIS SPACE TO JOURNAL ABOUT WHAT GOD IS SAYING TO YOU:

# DAY NINETY-ONE – JAMES 5:12

## SOMETHING TO STUDY:

*"Above all, my brothers, do not swear—not by heaven or by earth or by anything else. Let your 'Yes' be yes, and your 'No,' no, or you will be condemned."*
James 5:12

I love this verse because it talks about being men and women of integrity. You don't have to swear that something is true; you just need to tell the truth. Why do we have all these contracts? In the past your word was good enough. People would agree with a handshake because your words were your bond. Unfortunately, no one can trust each other anymore.

As I type this, I was booked to speak tonight for a youth convention in Minnesota. They had me booked for three years. I didn't send out a contract because I thought that our word should be enough. A week before the conference, I was informed that they had another speaker and would not be using me. They didn't care what was right; all they cared about was that they didn't have a signed contract from me so they were under no obligation. No obligation—except for their word and their accountability to God. The district guy said to me, "I hope that you learned something Greg." What I learned is that their word meant nothing and I can't trust them. It is a sad commentary today when the body of Christ will rip you off.

You need to be a person who says what they mean and means what they say. Let your "Yes" be yes and your "No" be no. Why is this important? Let me give you some reasons you should never lie or be deceptive.

- If your word doesn't mean anything, then you don't mean anything because you are your word. You must be men and women of character and integrity.

- Your trustworthiness is at stake. Take a beautiful vase and admire it. Now slam it on the floor and break it into hundreds of pieces. Next, paste it back together and make it look like new. How long would it take you to do that? It would take a really long time. This is what happens when you lie or are deceptive with your word. It will take a long time before people will believe and trust you again because you shatter your trustworthiness in their eyes when you lie. **Remember that love is unconditional, but trust is earned.** You develop trust by consistent behavior over a period of time. When you're untrustworthy, you cause a lot of confusion. People can't trust you or believe your word. It is going to take a while before others are going to believe you and whose fault is that? It is your fault!

- When you lie, you speak Satan's native tongue. You are speaking a language that the enemy loves and totally understands. John 8:44 says, *"You belong to your father, the devil, and you want to carry out your father's desire. He was a murderer from the beginning, not holding to the truth, for there is no truth in him. When he lies, he speaks his native language, for he is a liar and the father of lies."*

Since the devil is a liar and loves lies, we ought to be speaking the truth in love. Today telling the truth isn't that big of a deal to teenagers, but it is a huge deal for God. If you want Him to honor you, then you need to honor Him by telling the truth. When you lie, you make God look very bad! Your word is a reflection of you. Lying makes you look bad and people can't trust you. If you are a Christian, your word is also a reflection of God. Is God a liar? Would God ever lie to you? Do you ever wonder if you can trust God? NO, He is true to His word and we can trust Him completely. Therefore, people need to be able to trust what you say completely.

My children knew they would never get in more trouble than if they did these two things: disrespect their mother or lie.

- God hates a lying tongue. Proverbs 6:16 and 17b says, *"There are six things the Lord hates, seven that are detestable to him:...a lying tongue."* It makes sense to stay away from things that the Lord hates. What comes out of your mouth is important to the Lord and you are either going to tell the truth or you are going to lie; you are either trustworthy or undependable.

Your character is your guarantee that what you are saying is the truth. You don't need to swear to anything that you are telling the truth. You need to be so trustworthy that no oath or swearing is ever needed.

Be a person of such integrity that a contract would not need to be in place for something to happen. I will fill out contracts and sign them, but the fact is that no group needs a contract with me because my word is my bond and I will do exactly as I promised I would do.

Matthew 5:34-37 says, *"But I tell you, do not swear an oath at all: either by heaven, for it is God's throne; or by earth, for it is his footstool; or by Jerusalem, for it is the city of the Great King. And do not swear by your head, for you cannot make even one hair white or black. All you need to say is simply 'Yes' or 'No'; anything beyond this comes from the evil one."*

I also understand that there are evil men and contracts are needed or people will rip you off. The sad fact is that you can't trust some people today. Can people trust you? When you tell your parents that you are going somewhere, do you do what you said you would do or are you deceptive? Do you tell your teachers the truth? Do you ever cheat in school? Do you make up stories and make stuff better or worse than they really are when you are talking to your friends?

When you swear that you are telling the truth, you do not make things more believable, but you make yourself more suspicious. You imply that if you aren't swearing, you aren't really telling the truth. A person needs to say, "I swear that I am telling the truth," only if their character is in question.

When you are honest and trustworthy, you will draw people closer to Jesus Christ; but when you are dishonest, you will push people away from Christ. You are God's ambassador here on earth and people will judge Him by your actions. You either make God look very good or you make God look very bad.

## SOMETHING TO THINK ABOUT:

1. Can people trust you?

2. How important is it to tell the truth? Do you tell the truth?

3. God cares about what comes out of your mouth.

## SOMETHING TO PRAY ABOUT:

Ask God to show you how important it is to Him and to others to tell the truth. Tell God that you desire to speak the truth from now on. Ask Him for the courage and power to tell the truth even if it means getting in trouble.

## USE THIS SPACE TO JOURNAL ABOUT WHAT GOD IS SAYING TO YOU:

# DAY NINETY-TWO – JAMES 5:13

## SOMETHING TO STUDY:

*"Is any one of you in trouble? He should pray. Is anyone happy? Let him sing songs of praise."*
James 5:13

**If you are having problems, spend time with God and if you are happy, spend time with God.** In other words…spend time with God! All of us have problems and struggles in life. Jesus Christ wants you to cast all your cares on Him. Why? Because He cares deeply for YOU! He looks forward to spending time with you and He delights in answering your prayers and walking you through your problems. Just remember that when you are having problems, God wants to deal with you before He deals with the trouble. He wants to sharpen, correct and work with your life. The trouble is meant to build you and draw you closer to Him.

Are you happy? Is life going great? Are you excited about what is happening? If yes, then spend time with Jesus. Be thankful and sing praises to Him. We often find ourselves seeking God when life is tough and ignoring God when life is good. You would get real tired, real fast if people only came to you to get something and never thanked you or appreciated you. This is what we do to God—come to Him during the hard times and forget Him during the good times. Praise the Lord for good days and thank Him for all the ways He is working in and through you. Every day He is working in your life whether you see it or not. Every day He is protecting, leading and caring for you. Take time to praise Him.

When is the last time you sang songs of praise to Him? I speak for a lot of churches. When worship is taking place, I see many students standing, looking around and talking with their friends, but not singing. Why don't you worship and sing? Some excuses would be: I don't feel like it, life stinks, what will my friends think, the music is bad, I have a very poor voice, etc. You can add to the list, but this is a time to sing songs of praise to Jesus Christ. This is your opportunity to tell Jesus that you are thankful for everything He is doing for you. It is a chance to spend time with Him, just like prayer. One day we will all sing before His throne and now is a chance to warm up for that moment.

237

Remember that we exist to glorify Jesus Christ, so take advantage of all the time you have to spend with Him. Spend time with Him when life is hard and spend time with Him when life is good.

## SOMETHING TO THINK ABOUT:

1. Where do you turn when life gets really hard?

2. When is the last time you have lifted your voice to God in praise?

3. Are you thankful for everything the Lord has done for you? Have you told Him you appreciate everything He has done?

## SOMETHING TO PRAY ABOUT:

Are you having trouble? Cast your cares on Him right now. Then thank God for everything He has done. Tell Him that you will sing songs of praise to Him the next time you are part of a worship time.

## USE THIS SPACE TO JOURNAL ABOUT WHAT GOD IS SAYING TO YOU:

# DAY NINETY-THREE – JAMES 5:14

## SOMETHING TO STUDY:

*"Is any one of you sick? He should call the elders of the church to pray over him and anoint him with oil in the name of the Lord."*
James 5:14

Does God still heal today? The answer is absolutely, totally and without a doubt...YES! It is pretty clear that James is saying that you can be healed. I believe that here James is talking about being physically healed, but I believe it also applies to emotional and spiritual healing.

If you are sick, call the elders and ask them to pray for you. Ask them to anoint you with oil. When someone anoints you, they are anointing you for a purpose. That purpose can be to serve, to live for and to glorify Jesus Christ.

*"Ask and it will be given to you; seek and you will find; knock and the door will be opened to you. For everyone who asks receives; he who seeks finds and to him who knocks, the door will be opened. If you, then, though you are evil, know how to give good gifts to your children, how much more will your Father in heaven give good gifts to those who ask him!"* Matthew 7:7-8, 11.

*"If you believe, you will receive whatever you ask for in prayer,"* Matthew 21:22.

*"If you remain in me and my words remain in you, ask whatever you wish, and it will be given you,"* John 15:7.

*"Until now you have not asked for anything in my name. Ask and you will receive, and your joy will be complete,"* John 16:24.

However, He doesn't always answer the way we want Him to answer. He can say yes, no or wait. It is never fun when God says no, but it is for our own good. Instead of healing, God might choose to give you peace, joy and grace to learn from the sickness. In one week, I prayed for a good friend and she was miraculously healed, but another friend continues to suffer physically. Why? Because God knows what is best for each individual and will work in each of our lives in unique ways.

It is good for elders to pray for someone's healing, but you can also pray for healing. Maybe you have been given the gift of healing—check out 1 Corinthians 12:9, 28, 30. Even if you don't have the gift of healing, God may choose to work through you, at a certain time, with a certain individual, to heal them.

**Never be afraid to step out in faith to do what God is calling you to do.** He always answers prayer and He can work through a teenager just as easily and maybe easier than He can work through an adult. It is not about you; it is all about God. Just be available to be used by Him.

## SOMETHING TO THINK ABOUT:

1. Do you need healing? Have you considered calling the elders?

2. Have you ever considered that God could use you to bring healing?

3. Be willing to step out in faith to pray for healing.

## SOMETHING TO PRAY ABOUT:

Ask God to lay anyone on your heart that needs His healing touch. Begin to pray for those who are sick physically, emotionally and spiritually and ask God to heal them.

## USE THIS SPACE TO JOURNAL ABOUT WHAT GOD IS SAYING TO YOU:

# DAY NINETY-FOUR – JAMES 5:15

## SOMETHING TO STUDY:

*"And the prayer offered in faith will make the sick person well; the Lord will raise him up. If he has sinned, he will be forgiven."*
James 5:15

**Healing is never about our abilities, but about faith in God alone.** It is about trusting Him totally and completely. Faith believes that God can do what He has promised He would do. Faith is approaching the throne of grace in confidence and humility and making your request to God (Hebrews 4:15-16). If the prayer is according to His will, then you will see the Lord heal. Sometimes the Lord will heal the person immediately and sometimes the healing will come over a period of time.

I once prayed from the front in a youth rally. I prayed for students to be healed. A teenage guy, who had been deaf in one ear since childhood, experienced God's healing while I prayed. How cool is that? On a summer mission trip, a Scottish couple came to me and said, "The Lord told us that if you would pray for my wife, she would be healed." I had all the girls gather around the wife and touch her while the guys stood around the girls. I asked three students to pray out loud and asked God to heal her. As they prayed, God healed her instantly. I was asked to pray for a teenage boy that had slipped into a coma. I prayed for his healing and he never got any better and eventually went to be with the Lord. God, in His infinite wisdom, will heal some people and not heal others. Again, He knows what is best for each person! But we must be willing to step out in faith and ask God to make the sick well.

Doesn't the verse say that the prayer offered in faith WILL make the sick person well? Yes, but it needs to be according to God's will and not just man's desire. You must always take scripture as a whole and not pull verses out of context. 1 John 5:14 says, *"This is the confidence we have in approaching God: that if we ask anything according to his will, he hears us."*

It is not our prayers or oil that heals the person, it is God who raises them up. He is the healer and He can choose to work through us if He wants. Being used to heal someone should cause humility and not

241

pride in your life. If you use a pen to write a great paper for English, should the pen feel any pride in writing that book? No! The pen was merely a tool used by you If you desired, you could have used another pen. If God uses you to heal, be thankful, but don't get a big head.

Part of the healing process can be the confession of sin. I believe that sin has made some people sick. Read 1 Corinthians 11:27-30 and ask yourself what is making people sick and die? Here it was taking communion in an unworthy manner. What does that mean? Partly, it means to take communion without confessing your sins. Part of healing a person is inviting them to make right their relationship with Jesus Christ by confessing all known sin to Him. How is your relationship with Christ right now?

## SOMETHING TO THINK ABOUT:

1. Could sin be causing you to get sick?

2. God can choose to use any Christian, at any time, to heal someone.

3. Read John 14:12 and apply that to healing.

## SOMETHING TO PRAY ABOUT:

Ask God for boldness to step out in obedience to do whatever He asks you to do.

## USE THIS SPACE TO JOURNAL ABOUT WHAT GOD IS SAYING TO YOU:

# DAY NINETY-FIVE – JAMES 5:16

## SOMETHING TO STUDY:

*"Therefore confess your sins to each other and pray for each other so that you may be healed. The prayer of a righteous man is powerful and effective."*
James 5:16

Does this verse mean that you should share your deepest and darkest secrets with everyone? No, but it does mean that you need to make your relationships with others right. If you have sinned against someone, you need to go to them and repent. Tell them you were wrong and ask them to forgive you. Afterwards, ask if they would be willing to pray for you. This verse also means that you should go to a mature Christian whom you can trust and tell them of the sins that you are struggling with and ask them to pray for you.

Some of you who are reading this are sick emotionally, physically or spiritually because of sin in your life. You don't hear anyone really talk about this cause of sickness, but I believe it impacts a number of people. You need to confess those sins, in some cases those secret sins that no one knows about, so that you can be healed. Humble yourself before others and ask their forgiveness and prayers. Taking this step can be exactly what you need to do to experience healing in your life.

The prayer of a righteous person is powerful and effective not because they are a superstar, but because God is working in and through them in powerful ways. Do you know any righteous people? Ask them to pray for you. What about you? What kind of person are you? Are you a righteous person or are you a wicked person? Do you want to do an interesting study? Sure you do, read Proverbs chapters 10, 11 and 12. I want you to compare the righteous person to the wicked person. Here is some of what you will discover.

RIGHTEOUS PERSON:
- 10:6- Blessings will crown your head. God will pour out His blessing upon you as you seek to live a life that is honoring to Him.

- 10:7- The memory of you will be a blessing to others. How will people remember you in high school?
- 10:21- With your lips you are building others up and encouraging them.
- 10:31- From your lips will come wisdom. Others will seek you out for advice and counsel. You will be respected because of what you say and how you help others.
- 11:8- You are rescued from trouble. That doesn't mean you don't have any trouble, but it means that in the midst of the trouble God will take care of you and bring you through it safely.
- 11:18- Being righteous will bring you a reward both now and in the future.
- 12:2- You obtain favor with the Lord. There is no greater place to be than in a place of favor with God. He will open doors, take care of you, set up divine appointments and give you favor in the eyes of man.
- 12:7- Your house will stand firm. You will not be shaken because God is taking care of you. You have nothing to fear or worry about. Storms will come but they will not destroy you because your house is built on the rock of righteousness.
- 12:26- You are cautious in friendships because you understand that bad company corrupts good character. You become whom you hang around with. **You can't soar like an eagle if you are hanging with the turkeys.**
- 13:1- You hate what is false. You hate lies, false gods and whatever sets itself up against the Lord God Almighty! (This was a bonus verse from chapter 13).

WICKED PERSON:
- 10:3- Their cravings are never satisfied. The more they get the more they want and they are never truly satisfied. They are empty on the inside and never seem to find what they really need or desire.
- 10:6- The trouble that they cause with their mouth will eventually destroy them. Their mouth gets them in trouble because it is filled with lies and deceit.
- 10:7- Your name will rot. Eventually, it will disappear and no one will remember you anymore, or you are

remembered as someone who was sick, messed up and disgusting.

- 10:20- Your heart is of little value. What you take into your mind goes into your heart and out of the overflow of your heart you act and speak. So the wicked man has a heart that is sick and depraved.
- 10:25- Storms in life destroy the wicked. They have no foundation and their life is filled with fear and worry. They are always giving up and giving in to what is wrong.
- 10:28- Their hopes come to nothing. All their dreams and hopes for the future fall apart because their lives are so messed up and they are constantly making bad choices.
- 11:6- They are trapped by their own evil desires. What they thought was fun ends up to be a pit and trap that starts to destroy them. Evil desires control them and they no longer control their desires.
- 11:9- You end up destroying others with your mouth, you are a gossip and a slanderer. When you do this, you show yourself to be godless.
- 11:21- You will be punished. God is slow to anger, but He is a just God and one day the wicked will be punished. They will end up reaping exactly what they have sowed.
- 12:5- You can't trust this person because even their advice is deceitful.

I just hit a few verses, but I want you to read all three of those chapters and write down everything it says about a righteous person and a wicked person. Right now, whom do you resemble the most? Honestly, do you want to be a wicked person or a righteous person? Make the changes that you need to make now to live a righteous life and be known as a righteous person.

Does this mean you are perfect? No. If you sin and make mistakes, will you bring sickness on your life? No. We all make mistakes and choose poorly at times. The wicked man is choosing a lifestyle that seeks after sin. A wicked man is not one who falls on occasion; a wicked man has given himself to sin and no longer cares about God's opinion of him or what is right. Seek righteousness so that you can be healed and used by God to bring healing to others.

## SOMETHING TO THINK ABOUT:

1. Are you more like the wicked person or the righteous person?

2. Have you been sick? Is there any sin you need to confess?

3. Talk to a mature Christian about some of your struggles.

## SOMETHING TO PRAY ABOUT:

Tell God that you want to be a righteous person. Ask Him to reveal any sin in your life that you need to confess and make right. Ask Him to reveal any people that you need to apologize to and ask forgiveness from.

## USE THIS SPACE TO JOURNAL ABOUT WHAT GOD IS SAYING TO YOU:

# DAY NINETY-SIX – JAMES 5:17-18

## SOMETHING TO STUDY:

*"Elijah was a man just like us. He prayed earnestly that it would not rain, and it did not rain on the land for three and a half years. Again he prayed, and the heavens gave rain, and the earth produced its crop."*
James 5:17-18

Elijah is an excellent example of the power of God working through a righteous man. The cool thing is that Elijah was a person just like us. He was no better than what we can become in Jesus Christ. We look at some of the older heroes of the faith and think, "I could never be like they are." That is a lie! God is ready and willing to work through YOUR life just like He worked through Elijah's life. **You can be a hero of the faith and experience God working through you in amazing and powerful ways.**

Grab your Bible and read about Elijah in 1 Kings 17:1-6 and 18:41-45. You will see that Jesus also talks about this story in Luke 4:25. Here is a righteous man who prayed that it would not rain and it didn't rain for three and a half years. He prayed again and the Lord brought rain; the famine was stopped and crops were produced. Nothing is impossible for God to do. As we pray according to His will, we will see Him working through us.

The more you pray the more answer to prayer you will see which will encourage you to pray even more. Your faith will be built up and you will be trusting God to do great and mighty things.

What did Elijah do that set him up to be used by God is such great ways? He walked with God, talked with God, listened to God and was obedient to God. Is any of this beyond what you can do? Matthew 17:20b, *"I tell you the truth, if you have faith as small as a mustard seed, you can say to this mountain, 'Move from here to there and it will move'. Nothing will be impossible for you."* God can do great things through you as you step out in faith.

Did Elijah ever struggle? Yes, right after a great victory on Mt. Carmel he becomes afraid, discouraged and depressed. Elijah runs away from the threats of man and forgets the awesomeness of God. That is the wonderful thing about the men and women of scripture; they all struggled just like you and me. They all had their strengths and weaknesses just like you and me.

When we read about the rain coming, we sometimes forget that Elijah prayed seven times for the rain before it finally came. Don't be discouraged when you don't see immediate results. Wait on the Lord and trust Him to answer in His perfect timing. We want something to happen and we want it now, but God sees all of eternity and knows when something needs to happen. So pray and wait on your God to answer.

## SOMETHING TO THINK ABOUT:

1. What great things do you trust God for right now?

2. Is God able to work through your life? What do you need to do to be a clean vessel for the Lord to use?

3. Elijah was a person just like YOU!

## SOMETHING TO PRAY ABOUT:

Ask God for faith to trust Him for great things. Listen to Him and be still before your King. What does God want you to ask of Him? Step out in faith and ask!

## USE THIS SPACE TO JOURNAL ABOUT WHAT GOD IS SAYING TO YOU:

# DAY NINETY-SEVEN – JAMES 5:19-20

## SOMETHING TO STUDY:

*"My brothers, if one of you should wander from the truth and someone should bring him back, remember this: Whoever turns a sinner from the error of his way will save him from death and cover over a multitude of sins."*
James 5:19-20

There are several things that I want you to pay attention to in these verses. First of all, this is a Christian who has fallen. This is your brother or sister in Christ who has made some bad choices. He or she is part of your youth group and has done well in the past, but isn't doing well now.

Second of all, notice that this person is wandering from the truth and is in error. Things that they had believed were true, things they were taught and even things they had taught others are now no longer a part of their life. They have allowed their feelings to deceive them and they believe that what they are doing will fulfill them more than Jesus will. These people are pursuing, living in, and seeking after sin.

What do you do? Do you judge them, gossip about them, criticize them and reject them? No, you seek them out in love and you speak truth into their lives. You care enough about your Christian family that you are now going to do something. **Your love as a Christian needs to move you to action.**

It is not about us convincing or debating this person back to the Lord. It is all about us praying for them, loving them and reaching out to them. It is allowing the Holy Spirit to work through us to draw them back to the arms of Jesus.

By doing this, you will save them from a spiritual, emotional and maybe physical death. The wages of sin is death. Sin first kills us on the inside emotionally and spiritually; our heart begins to harden and we no longer care about what we are doing and how it is impacting God, others or us. If we allow the sin long enough, it even has the power to kill us physically.

What is the truth and how can we tell if someone is wandering? The truth is the Word of God and that is our final authority for life and living. To wander from the truth of Scripture is to wander from God Himself. It is important that we win the lost to Christ, but it is also important to win the saved back to Christ. Be sure that you follow the guidelines spelled out in Matthew 18:15-17 if they are involved in sin.

- Go to them one to one. If they don't listen, then take step two.
- Take one or two others with you and confront them again in love. If they still don't listen, take step three.
- We tell the Church.

Our goal is to see our brother or sister in Christ loving and living for Jesus just like we are doing right now! Right? Right!

## SOMETHING TO THINK ABOUT:

1. Do you need to talk to someone who has wandered from the truth?

2. Before you talk with anyone else, be sure that you are right before the Lord!

3. We need to love our friends enough to risk our relationship with them.

## SOMETHING TO PRAY ABOUT:

Ask God to bring those who have wandered, back to Him. Tell Him you will go.

## USE THIS SPACE TO JOURNAL ABOUT WHAT GOD IS SAYING TO YOU:

# CONCLUSION

Thank you for taking this journey through James. I hope that you have a greater knowledge of God's Word, a closer walk with the Lord, and a better understanding of His desires for your life. Remember that there is nothing more important than your walk with Jesus Christ!

# CONTACT INFORMATION

I would love to hear from you. If you have any questions or if I can encourage you, please feel free to contact me at:

Gregospeck@gmail.com

On Facebook – be my friend!

Twitter @Gregospeck

Web Site – http://www.gregspeck.com

Made in the USA
Lexington, KY
13 November 2019